By Aaron Scardina and Kevin Whelan

The Suck of Work

Acknowledgements

First and foremost, we'd like to thank the people that hired us for every shitty job we've ever had (which would be all of them, since "shitty job" is redundant). If it weren't for the years of miserable employment, this amazing work of art would not have been possible. We wish to thank Brainyquote.com for having an extensive database of quotes and easy to navigate site. We'd like to thank our parents for not having enough money to let us be pampered, irresponsible playboys, and our siblings for going through it with us. It is unthinkable to imagine a life devoid of the joy of working for minimum wage. Finally we must thank our women folk for all their help and support, including but not limited to their proofreading, feedback, encouragement, food, and sex. They say behind every great man there is a great woman. Well sometimes there's great women behind mediocre men.

Table of Contents

Welcome to your new job.
HELP US!
RUN!
SAVE YOURSELF!

Introduction

"The only place success comes before work is in the dictionary."
- Vince Lombardi
And so does "suck."

Dedication

This book is dedicated to all those who must work for a living. It is written for the brave schmoes who go out and try to earn a paycheck while hating every single minute of it. It's for all who must wake up, day after day, week after week, year after year, and drag ourselves to hours of torture because we must. We must because we see no other way to provide the necessities of life to self and family. For those of you who actually enjoy your work or don't need to work, go blow a goat. When you're finished, clean up, find the nearest working schmoe, and give them your money.

Disclaimer

First of all, why does no one ever write a "claimer?" I think that would show some balls to say something like, “Go ahead and try some of this shit yourself. We take full responsibility for giving you some really bad ideas, and we hope you're dumb enough to try them! Our goal is to assist natural selection." But it's a sue-happy world, and no one wants to lose their money and stuff. We don't either, so here's our disclaimer: This book was written by professionals...no, that's not correct. This book was written by lazy schmoes. Any suggestions we make are probably bad ideas, so we wouldn't advise you actually do any of the things described in this book. If you do, you do it at your own risk to life, liberty, and the pursuit of whatever. Also, try to get it on video for others to enjoy.

Lower Your Expectations

This book is not going to make your job better. We're not going to fill your heads with inspirational ideas or ways to delude yourself into thinking your job isn't that bad. We aren't going to give you useful tips on how to find happiness in your work. We know it sucks, and it will probably continue to suck. We merely want to say that we understand, and that hopefully this book will provide you with some laughs in the midst of your misery. We also hope you and everyone you know buys the book so we don't have to work anymore.

Definitions

Before you go any further into this book, we must define a few key phrases for the purpose of understanding:

Job - Bad place you go to trade life for money.
Career - A commitment to give even more of your life away.
Work - That stuff you do at a job or career which sucks immeasurably.
Job Description - A summary of the shit you're always getting yelled at for not doing.
Schmoe - He or she who must endure this wretched invention known as work, and who often must do it for a great portion of their lives, deriving little satisfaction or enjoyment from the process.
BOSS - Acronym for Big Ol' Sack of Shit, AKA manager, supervisor.
Coworker - A fellow schmoe in the trenches.
Living - That thing you try to "make" but rarely do.
Laziness - Natural human reaction to having to do something that sucks.

The Part of the Schmoe

Once you begin down the path to schmoe-dom it can be difficult, if not impossible, to break free. I feel like I've been typecast as a schmoe. It's like when an actor plays the same type of part over and over again. I did well at my first job and now I have been pigeonholed into that part again and again. Actors, to avoid being typecast, will stretch themselves and go for a role that is 180 degrees from their typical role. So how does a schmoe go about doing the same thing? I mean if you are a good worker and did a 180, then your work ethic goes out the window. That doesn't help you land a better job or role. Nope, in fact, it may be even shittier than before. Let's face it, you're typecast from the minute you fill out your first application. And...that's a wrap.

Chapter 1

Looking for a Job

"To find out what one is fitted to do, and to secure an opportunity to do it, is the key to happiness."

- John Dewey

Too bad most of us just get wedged in and stuck somewhere.

Job searching

At some point a job search is required. If you don't have much in the skills department it can be a very frustrating and depressing task. When you look at the available jobs it almost seems to be a list of things you CAN'T do. Wow! Look at all these jobs that I'm dangerously unqualified for!

Trying to find a schmoe job can be much like shopping for underwear in a thrift store. You don't want them to begin with, you're unlikely to find a good fit, and there's leftover DNA from the last person who, probably for good reason, didn't want them anymore.

The best way to get a decent job is to know someone. Everyone knows this but it's the knowing people with any power that's the difficult part. I know a lot of people and those people would actually prevent me from getting a decent job.

Job Description Doubletalk

Job listings are laden with bullshit and you have to learn how to sift through it. If the job sounds too good to be true, it is. If you see, "must enjoy loud music," or "must like to have fun," you can be pretty certain there will be none of either. There might not even be a real job.

Often you will see things like “competitive wages” advertised. This is supposed to entice the reader, but all it really means is that their pay is in line with other crappy wages in that category. You never see “obscenely higher wages than deserved” advertised, but that would be nice.

Another funny description is “seasonal” or “summer” job. These code words tend to mean that, "We reserve the right to pay low wages without benefits, schedule shitty hours, and lay you off whenever we feel like it."

Seasonal work puts you in a unique position, especially if you don't plan on trying to get the job again the next year. You already know from the start that the job will end soon, regardless of your performance, so there's no need to fear job loss. Enjoy this freedom and give them "seasonal effort." Show up late, move slowly, and sip lemonade. Tell your boss the work will get done when it gets done. Or it won't.

Tweaking the Suck

If you even have a choice when choosing a job, the goal is to have it suck the least amount possible. It is inevitable that it will suck to some degree, so all you can really do is try to tweak that suck. The total suck factor of a job is the sum of all job variables. If you keep things like workload and responsibility minimal while maximizing pay and perks, you may be able to reach a tolerable suck factor. However, other unforeseen variables pop up that can tweak the suck. You might walk into a job you think you can deal with only to find that your boss is a super dick. Bam! Just like that the suck factor goes way up. Conversely, you may think you're in a situation you can barely tolerate until you find out you will be in close proximity to a sexy coworker. Bloop! Suck factor goes down a few notches. But in the end, unfortunately, it all still adds up to "suck."

Recruitment

Any employer that must resort to recruitment for low-level jobs should be avoided. If a company is having trouble finding employees that's a pretty obvious sign that it sucks to work there. The only possible exception is when a new business opens and they need a bunch of workers at once. But it’s still probably better to steer clear and let other saps be the guinea pigs. Recruitment is best left to the military. At least with them you know going in that misery and the risk of death are guaranteed.

Job Fairs

When you think of a fair, you think of rides, food, games, fun, etc. A job fair, on the other hand, is a room full of people representing companies with job openings so shitty they had to set up there. Despite its lack of deep-fried foods and spinning rides, a job fair still manages to give you the urge to vomit. A plethora of recruiters and prospective applicants attempting to "network" by putting forth their best contrived politeness can induce nausea in almost anyone. Sorry kids, no T-shirts, shorts, or funnel cakes. Just suits, ties, and sweaty handshakes.

Nepotism

Ahhh, nepotism. If it weren't for nepotism, how would our government function? Of course, nepotism is rampant in the private sector. Your stance on the subject probably has a lot to do whether you've benefited from it or been screwed by it. If you're the niece of CEO Uncle Remington, good for you. Life tossed you a bone. Just watch your back, because the other more qualified people who didn't get the job are pissed off and may own weapons.

I for one, am thankful for nepotism because it gave us bands like the Jackson Five. It's hard for me to imagine a world without "Dancing Machine." I also support it in the case of sexy, related women, especially twins.

Equal Opportunity Employment

I suppose this might be a good concept, but like most ideals, exists only in theory. Like it or not, many people hold various prejudices, sometimes without even realizing it. But do we truly want equal opportunity employment? I think a little prejudice comes in handy from time to time. For example, do we really want Akmed the Jihadist working with us in the bomb factory? He may be the most qualified for the job, but there's probably a reason for that we won't like. And who wants to walk into a strip club and get a lap dance from a 70-year-old 350-pound former sumo champ? Okay, maybe a few of you, but they can have a special night for that.

Surveys & Articles

Feel like some useless info? Well, read an article online regarding work. You'll see things like, "Top 10 Jobs That Make People Happy." On that list, examples might include CEO, executive V.P., successful rock musician, adult film star, and professional golfer. You, reading the article, realize that you are not any of those things and don't have the means to ever be any of those things. Ditto for articles like; "5 Jobs That Pay 500k a Year!" Hey, check out what I can do after a brain transplant and ten years of schooling!

Things to Consider When Reading An Article About Work

Who is the author and what makes his or her advice matter? Before you read the actual article, the first thing to do is go directly to the bottom and read about the author. You are likely to find some odd description of what makes them qualified to write such an article. You'll see something like: "Tim Tallywacker is a job search and social media consultant, a career and life coach, author, speaker, and resume writer." Sounds like a fancy description for unemployed to me. This person doesn't even have a real job but he is telling you and me how to get one. Fuck that! Tell me how not to work. You seem to be pulling that off quite well, write about how you did it you greedy prick!

Is the information practical and usable? You'll see a headline online that reads; "10 Ways to Make a Job You Hate More Tolerable." At this point you are at the end of your rope anyway, so why not read the article? Then you open the article and read preposterous suggestions. "Ask your supervisor for an unpaid leave for 8 weeks for a mental health getaway." The second you read it, you know you can't come close to pulling off any of the writer's suggestions. Yet again you were fooled into reading a useless article written by a clueless jackass.

Maybe the writers are giving bad advice on purpose to thin the herd for themselves. If the info provided seems a little far-fetched then maybe they are trying to get you to fail. Perhaps the article gives some advice on what to do at an interview. They might say, "Your goal is to be noticed and stand out among the pack at the interview. You need to grab their attention in the first 30 seconds or else they may see you as ordinary. Show up with your cock out and a post it note on the tip reading, "I'm your man." Yeah try that and see what happens.

Chapter 2

Applying for a Job

"I have always advised people never to apply for a job you do not really want."

- Michael Todd

If everyone followed that advice, the need for job applications would be eliminated.

Required Paperwork

You can generally gauge the level of job you are applying for by what type of paperwork is required. If you are simply asked to fill out an application and you are handed a pen that's been chewed on, it's most likely a crappy minimum wage job. If they ask you to submit a resume, we can be pretty certain you're not going to be bussing tables or stocking shelves. You will likely be subjected to a slightly more sophisticated form of job suckitude. However, if you are required to have an impressive and extensive portfolio, you will probably make lots of money and won't be reading this book. You're too busy handing down policies for schmoes to follow.

Job Application Questions

Some of the questions on a job application are ridiculous. For example, "Are you eligible to work in the United States?" If I am someone like an illegal alien that underwent untold trials and tribulations to get into the country to find work, am I going to sell myself out on a job application? I probably can't even fill one out.

How about, "Have you ever been convicted of a felony? If yes, explain." Well let me get right on that. Sit back and relax while you read all about my criminal escapades and then decide not to hire me. Why don't we stop wasting people's time and just put a little note on the top of the application: “Don't bother applying if you've spent time in the slammer or came to this country in the back of a van by the cover of night.”

Sample Resumes

Many jobs require resumes, but there are quite a few opportunities that generally don't. Although if they did, we’d imagine that some of them might look like the following:

Homeless Guy

Name: Most people call me "Homeless Guy"
Address: Changes daily

Objective

To remain unemployed at this time. I can't be reached or anything but I appreciate you looking over my resume.

Experience

2006 - 3:37PM: Walked aimlessly with my cart finding the best places to beg, eat, pee, and sleep. Muttered to myself incoherently and screamed of injustice to random people on the street.
2005: Escaped from Fearsome Pines Mental Facility.
2003 - 2004: Put away for psychological evaluations.
2002: Started drinking wildly, lost my job, and stopped paying bills. Called my wife a bitch at a PTA meeting. Lost my kids when she moved away.
2001: Caught woman of my dreams having sex with coworker.
1996 - 2000: Married to the woman of my dreams. Had two beautiful children, a nice house, good friends, and a great job.

Skills

Excellent shouting voice
Walking
Fixing shopping carts
Dumpster diving
Discreet on-street defecation

Education

Ph.D. from the street

References

Joe down at the soup kitchen, pigeons, that girl I follow, historical figures, Ed

Mobster

Vinny Cappuchino
Where I live doesn't concern you

Objective

To get in on the ground floor of a respectable crime family as a low level thug with potential for advancement.

Highlights

Proficient in grabbing crotch and saying "Eh."
Never ratted out any friends.
Love spaghetti and other Italian foods.
Enjoy listening to Frank Sinatra.
Fingerprints burnt off in molotov cocktail accident.

Education

Repeated viewings of Goodfellas, Casino, and The Godfather Trilogy.
Shadowed the school bully to learn about ass-beatings.

Experience

Sold stolen cigarettes to classmates in grade school.
Had multiple students and teachers paying me their lunch money for "protection."
Played little league to learn how to properly swing a baseball bat.
Carried out hits on noisy neighborhood pets.

References

Frankie One-Ball
Lasangna Louie
Most of the broads from the neighborhood

Terrorist

Abtuba Firawahtah-Goldstein
1383 Blood of the Serpent Lane
Tora Bora, Afghanistan

Objective
Seeking to help bring about the coming of the 12th Imam and a swift, but painful, death to all non-believers. However, more immediately I am pursuing a career that allows me to maximize my skill set with a potential for growth and development.

Experience
2007 - Present: Professor of explosives and bomb making at University of the Cave. (Go U of C!)
2001 - 2006: Hunted and killed hundreds of lying evil infidels like dogs in the street. The street that runs red with blood!
1998 - 2000: Organized the terrorist cell, Allah Beckons Bastards Away (A.B.B.A.). Incidentally, we didn't know about the band with the same name.
1995 - 1997: Worked as an intern with Al-Queda, where I fetched tea, trimmed beards, and refitted sandals.

Education
Bachelors in Intolerance Engineering
Minor in Restaurant Management

References
Most are dead but here are a few:
Ma and Pa Firawahtah
Aziz Sadar - Al-Queda's #1 leader (formally # 4, 3, & 2)
Jimmy Carter

Prostitute

Trixie Styles
3rd and Broadway

Objective
To have a lucrative career of exchanging sexual favors for money under the protection of a benevolent pimp.

Education
Watched a lot of porn.
Experience
WAY more than average for a female my age.

Achievements and Awards
Youngest in class to lose virginity.
Voted biggest slut in high school.
Champion of local strip club's ping pong ball distance contest three years running.

Computer Skills
Can type with toes while web chatting.
Able to accept payment from johns through PayPal.

Special Skills
Can deep throat 12-inch kielbasa
Able to do anal without lube
Can withstand pimp slaps without showing visible bruises

Note: References withheld for confidentiality purposes

10 Dream Jobs That Should Exist

1. Vice President of Procrastination
2. Afternoon Nap Quality Controller
3. Problem Ignorer
4. Yard Ornament Demolisher
5. Time Wasting Specialist
6. Owner of Monkey Businesses
7. Pastry Consumption Expert
8. Brassiere Removal Assistant
9. Urine Based Snow Calligrapher
10. Executive of Questionable Taste

Chapter 3
Interviews

"To do a really good interview, you have to be truly interested in the person."

- Daisy Fuentes

That might help explain why I've had so many shitty interviews.

Visual Inspection

If I were an employer, I could understand the desire to meet and speak with someone before I hired them. It certain cases it provides for easy elimination. For example, if a guy walks in with a visible knife, no shirt, and a swastika tattoo on his forehead, it's probably safe to say you won't hire him. Then again, if you need security for KKK meetings, he may be the ideal candidate.

Interview Questions

A large problem with interviews are the questions asked. The interviewer sets out to find the most qualified person for the job (or the best-looking), but usually ends up hiring the best bullshitter. You cannot ask ridiculous and impractical questions and then expect honest answers. All that can be deciphered from these questions is how good you can think on your feet and how well you can lie.

An interview is like a first date, you are both on your best behavior. You are hoping you are going to get laid but usually you have to go out 2 or 3 more times before that happens. If you get the job, then you scored. But as with most bad relationships things change and you get tired of seeing that same person every day. You have to break up and do it all over again.

Sample Interview Q & A

Below is an incomplete list of interview questions that might come up during the interview with a potential employer. We all know that if you're really trying to get the job, you feed them the bullshit they want to hear rather than what you're really thinking.

So tell me about yourself?

The Expected Bullshit:

I'm a self-motivated team player who enjoys challenges and a fast-paced work environment.

What You're Thinking:

Can you possibly ask a more vague question?

Why are you the best person for the job?

The Expected Bullshit:

I am highly qualified, diligent, and eager to learn.

What You're Thinking:

I'm the best liar you've talked to so far.

Why did you leave your last job?

The Expected Bullshit:

There was no opportunity for advancement and I felt that I did everything that I could. I'm seeking new challenges with a well-established leader in the field like your company.

What You're Thinking:

It really sucked.

How would you describe the pace at which you work?

The Expected Bullshit:

Quickly and efficiently while still maintaining attention to detail.
What You're Thinking:
Just fast enough not to get fired.

Where do you see yourself in five years?
The Expected Bullshit:
Hopefully still working my way up the corporate ladder, having amply demonstrated my usefulness and strong work ethic to the company.
What You're Thinking:
Shit if I know.

What problems have you encountered at work?
The Expected Bullshit:
I've encountered a range of workplace-related difficulties, from coworker disagreements to natural disasters, but we always managed to pull together as a team and get through them.
What You're Thinking:
The usual kind of stuff. Getting there on time, staying there all day, doing work while I'm there, etc.

How do you feel about working long hours and weekends?
The Expected Bullshit:
Whatever it takes to get the job done. Work isn't just about a paycheck to me. It's about stepping up to the plate when your company needs you.
What You're Thinking:
I don't feel good about that at all. I don't even like working part-time let alone overtime.

How do you handle stress and pressure?
The Expected Bullshit:

I thrive under pressure. I set my priorities, delegate tasks, and remain calm.
What You're Thinking:
I go into the restroom with a bottle of Jack and shiver naked in the corner with the lights out.

What led you to this point in your life?
The Expected Bullshit:
It's been a combination of hard work, determination, and the desire to achieve.
What You're Thinking:
Everything that happened before this interview, pretty much, led me here.

Did you ever postpone making a decision? Why?
The Expected Bullshit:
Yes, because I felt that there wasn't enough information available at the time to make an informed choice.
What You're Thinking:
Yes I have postponed a decision because I wanted to make it later. Doing it now would've conflicted with that decision.

Give an example of how you motivated your coworkers or employees?
The Expected Bullshit:
I used a combination of positive reinforcement and goal setting to achieve the desired results.
What You're Thinking:
Shooting a gun wildly at their feet seems to work for most people. Others, I just buy them doughnuts.

Lastly, do you have any questions for me?
The Expected Bullshit:

What can I expect after this interview?
What You're Thinking:
Just one. What's up with all these stupid questions?

10 More Dream Jobs That Should Exist

1. Couch Sitter
2. Authorized Line Cutter
3. Secretary of Chocolate Ingestion
4. Panty Mechanic
5. CEO of Hanging Out
6. Clerk of Chicanery
7. Dean of Lying Around
8. Abstinence Prevention Associate
9. Unprofessional Driver on an Open Course
10. Flatulence Ignition Technician

chapter 4

Passing the Tests

"Be open to the amazing changes which are occurring in the field that interests you."

- Lee Steinberg

In other words, find out what new drugs you will be tested for.

Physicals

Before you get the green light to start your job, you might actually have to get a physical. That is a good indication that this will NOT be a desk job. I remember once I had four physicals scheduled in one week for different companies. So basically, I had my nuts in the hands of four people, not including my girlfriend, that week. Each doctor happened to be an old male as well. Isn't that weird though? Here I am just trying to get a job and he's fidgeting with my sack. Where's the connection? Is there one? Apparently while handling my testicles, he's looking for a reason why I can't work. It almost feels like the doctor is blind and he is reading the bumps on my balls, like it's braille. "Hmm, strong able man, yes to work!"

Background Checks

What happened to letting bygones be bygones, water under the bridge, leaving the past behind us and all that shit? Everyone has made a few mistakes in their life. Being arrested for drugs doesn't make me incapable of delivering them. It makes me the victim of a stupid law. Underage drinking could simply mean I was ahead of my time. Murderers, rapists, and the like notwithstanding, why do we jump to the conclusion that not having a criminal record is a good thing? Maybe you don't have one because you're a big pussy afraid to take chances and have fun. Oh yeah, I guess that IS what they want.

Drug Tests

Along the same lines as a physical are drug tests. They take your urine at a certain location, then send it to a lab to see if you are drug free enough to work. Wow, I'm amazed at what pee can do! Now if it does come back positive (because you need pot now and then to cope with how mundane and monotonous your job is) just tell them your pee took the drugs, not you. Hey if they are going to test the pee for drugs, then BLAME the pee FOR the drugs! “You know I told my urine several times to quit smoking. Man, my pee pisses me off sometimes!” It’s just a shame that something as unimportant as human waste can keep you from something important, like making a living.

Ways to Beat Drug Tests

- Stop doing drugs. People forget that this often works.
- Bribe the nurse with the drugs you’re using.
- Send someone that looks like you to take the test.
- Flush your system by consuming random, FDA-unapproved herbal shit that makes wild, unsubstantiated claims and probably destroys your liver.
- Acquire substitute pee. Some options for getting this include hanging out in an elementary school bathroom, harvesting some used diapers (baby or adult), or wringing out bedsheets from a nursing home. If you use this method, just try to make sure the donor is clean. You don’t want to dodge getting caught for pot only to get busted for heroin.

Chapter 5

Mornings

"The brain is a wonderful organ; it starts working the moment you get up in the morning and does not stop until you get into the office."

-Robert Frost

Or it doesn't start working at all.

Dreaming You're At Work

As if being at work all day isn't bad enough, sometimes you work in your sleep. The misery of work has manifested itself into horrible "workmares," not unlike the effects of post-traumatic stress disorder. In these dreams nothing seems to go right and you are powerless to stop it. As a result, instead of waking up refreshed and rested, you arise a sweaty ball of stress dreading the day ahead. I say take the day off because, in a sense, you've already worked. Explain to your boss that you're not coming in because you were on the midnight shift.

Dream Destroyer

Not only can work wreak havoc on your nighttime dreams, it destroys your dreams of a better life. It does this slowly and methodically, like water eroding solid rock. Except people aren't really like rocks, they're more like pliable squishy things that are easily smashed.

At age 20, I wanted to do standup comedy for a living. By age 30, I was glad I was still living and able to stand up. In my younger years I thought I had a fairly clear picture of what I wanted to do with my life. As I get older, however, it seems the only knowledge I gain is knowing exactly what I don't want to do.

I'd like to know who came up with the phrase, "You can do anything if you put your mind to it." No, not really. I don't care how hard you put your mind to it, there's just some shit you are never going to be able to do. Parents and teachers need to stop filling kids' heads with this bullshit. Better to have at least a semi-realistic idea of your limitations so you can save yourself some time and embarrassment. I'm not saying never try anything. I'm saying don't think you're going to be an astronaut just because you like to wear helmets.

Snooze Button

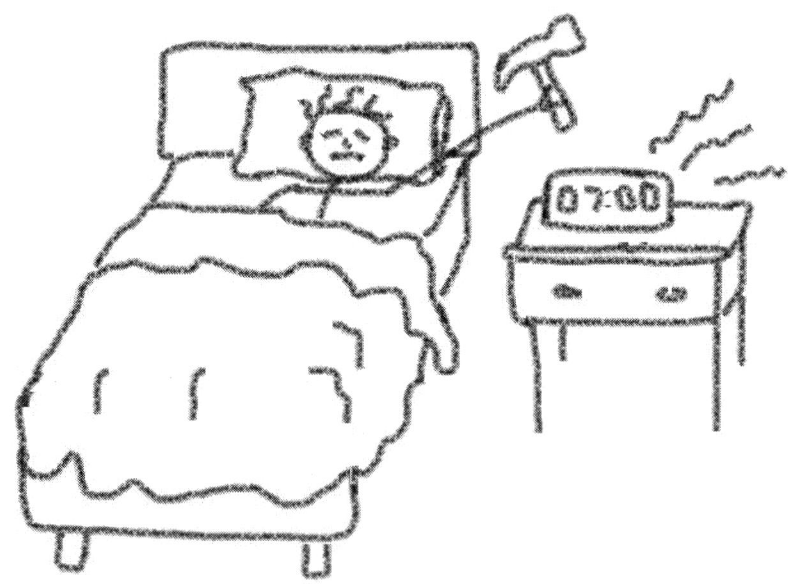

Nine more minutes of sleep. That's what the snooze button provides when you push it. What a powerful concept that is.

Push and sleep. It's procrastination at the touch of a button. The more tired you are, the more you push it, and the more morning rituals you subtract from your routine. "Hmmm, I can get away with not shaving today." Bam! Hit the snooze bar. "How badly do I really need a shower?" Bam! Hit it again. So on down the list you go eliminating preparations until you eventually find yourself driving ninety miles an hour to work hungry, smelly, and not wearing pants.

Working With Insomnia

Hi my name is Kevin and I'm an insomniac. I've been an insomniac for eight years now. Insomnia is a natural reaction to going against the grain. It's your body's way of telling you that it wants to do something else. If you ignore the message, you're bound to suffer...and be awake for it. Your body is trying to get your attention but you are too tired to notice.

The bottom line is you can't sleep but you still have to get up and go to work. You know, the place that started your sleep issues to begin with. It's when you are at your worst that you get fucked with the most by customers, coworkers, and bosses. The suck gets cranked up a notch and seems to be more in your face. Of course while you are there, you feel you could drop instantly and sleep for 12 hours.

Your Life in 1/3rds.

In an ideal life full of balance and happiness, the following is supposed to occur. You work for 8 hours, sleep for 8 hours and spend the other 8 hours doing your own thing. That sounds perfect doesn't it? However, we all know it doesn't work that way.

You have to borrow some time from either your personal time or sleep time to get up and get to work and take some more time for the ride home. But if you're miserable at work then that time will affect the rest of your day as well. Maybe you can't sleep due to stress of the day or the anxiety of tomorrow. So now the time set aside for sleep is getting shredded.

From the time you get off work until you lay down should be your time to relax and enjoy yourself...but you are too tired and spent from doing something you hate all day. Not only that, but there's housework and other chores to do that cut into more of your free time. Have you noticed that the only time that never seems to be affected is your work time? That 8 hours is rigid, unwavering, and steadfast and cannot, shall not, be fucked with. Forget that you're killing yourself slowly, becoming depressed, and a drag to be around. So much for work/life balance!

10 Signs You Are Working in a Better Job Than Before

1. No one seems to call you “Hoss” anymore.
2. You are above ground and sitting is permissible.
3. There is climate control other than dirty box fans.
4. The bathroom isn't portable and is separated according to gender.
5. The shit you deal with is just figurative now.
6. Coworkers speak English.
7. Your clothing is not made of paper and doesn't require a hat.
8. You no longer have to read or sign paperwork for illiterate coworkers.
9. No longer have to ask the guard to loosen the chain so you can scratch your wounds.
10. You don't need flashlights, helmets, gas masks, Hazmat suits, calluses, goggles, or a high tolerance for unbearable pain to do your job.

Chapter 6

Starting a Job

"There is no substitute for hard work."

- Thomas A. Edison

Sure there is. There's the lottery, crime, gold digging, mooching, ...and soybeans. Soybeans are always a good substitute.

Orientation

Before you actually start a new job, you might have to attend an orientation to get you familiar with the company and their policies. Some places go for very basic information. I was watching a video that explained that we should "shower often with soap and wear deodorant." Me? I was insulted but other people were taking notes, so who knows? I guess some people need that type of information. "Please refrain from racial slurs and unwarranted sexual advances." Who is this for? Was someone in that room watching that video having their plans thwarted in that moment? "Aw man!"

Orientation and any other type of on-the-job training is rooted in political correctness. We learn how to treat people and how NOT to treat people from our parents and probably Sesame Street. Yet for some reason we have to go through these PC meetings just in case, we adults, have forgotten our manners or are total idiots. Orientation is sterile, neutral, corporate, and a complete waste of time.

Training

Training isn't always an accurate term for the time you spend learning how to do your job. Often you get thrown right in without being taught a damn thing because no one wants to deal with the fresh meat. They figure you're probably going to quit anyway so you're not worth the effort. They don't even want to learn your name, unless of course, you're attractive.

At the other end of the spectrum, you are put through endless training procedures that involve videos, brochures, booklets, tests, observation, practice, simulations, and countless other bullshit. The irony here is that often after all that, you still don't know how to do the job.

First Days

A great way to offset the stress of starting a new job is to revel in the fact that you have license to fuck up. People don't expect much from you because you're new. It's a good time...unless you are hired with an overachiever. Then you have to be on your game to impress. Unfortunately, if you are genetically incapable of impressing people, there will be a clear distinction between the two of you. That person will shine and you will look like a schmuck.

Probationary Periods

When you start some jobs, you are immediately on probation for a certain period of time. Isn't that backwards, like guilty until proven innocent? They are basically saying, "We're going to assume you're a shithead until you prove otherwise." I can understand wanting to figure out if someone is a good worker, but isn't probation something you're supposed to get AFTER you do something bad?

If you start a new job and they place you on probation, let them know you are placing THEM on probation as well. Tell them you'll be watching them very closely, keeping tabs on their performance. Make sure they understand you will be checking their compliance with the law and will report any unsafe or unfair labor practices. Do your best to make them afraid of YOU.

Trusting People at Work

At a new job you maintain your best behavior for the first several months. It's really nothing more than the extension of your "interview" persona. After that period, you are able to cut the shit and be more open to your coworkers. But first, you have to find out who you can trust. That is something that takes finesse. You can't ask people you just met if they smoke pot, like anal sex, etc. You have to ease people down that road to see if they can handle that type of talk. It's time for your own kind of interview, a pervert test, so to speak. Mention something you read (even if its total bullshit) to get their reaction. That reaction will let you know if you can drop the fake and get real. "Hey Lori, did you see that article online about pot smokers who like casual sex? Isn't that crazy?" Then you study her reactions and listen intently for the reply. If she comes back with something along the lines of, "yeah I wrote it" then you are golden. It's time to ask her out for drinks.

10 Signs You Are Working in a Worse Job Than Before

1. There are armed guards making sure no one escapes.
2. Your new coworkers are under 10 and heavy on the Asian side.
3. Payment is made in company money that can only spent on non-beatings.
4. Light is provided by torches.
5. You can't recall a formal interview, just being rounded up and everything going black.
6. When asking where the bathroom is, you are handed a shovel.
7. You are blindfolded when taken to your work location.
8. Furniture is made from human bones.
9. Posters on the wall read, “Don't call them tumors, call them friends!”
10. You are shackled to your work area.

Chapter 7

Dressing for Work

"Beware of all enterprises that require a new set of clothes."
- Henry David Thoreau
That's right. I can work just fine in my old shit.

Uniforms

Uniforms sounds like unicorns. Unfortunately, they're not nearly as cool but just as gay. Uniforms are an unfashionable way of saying, "I surrender my individuality, mind, and free thought to this company." It is handy that you don't have to think about what to wear to work, but you can see that this is one more way your job destroys your brain's ability to think for itself.

Some uniforms are practical and conservative whereas others can make you feel one step away from the circus. I'm not knocking the circus, I'm just saying you shouldn't have to dress like a clown unless you are actually in it. Peanuts, anyone?

Some places don't even have the decency to give you a new uniform. Employee turnover is so high you get hand-me-downs from a previous victim. If you're lucky you'll get a uniform from someone who bathed regularly, although it might still come with pit stains and cigarette burns.

Work Clothes

A portion of your budget has to go towards buying clothing for work. Some places have a dress code that you must follow. If your previous place of employment was any different, time to buy new clothes to be deemed acceptable by your new work environment. You can't possibly do your job in jeans and a T-shirt if you work at an office! Are you kidding me? You regress into a barbarian in that attire! You need slacks, baby, slacks! Creased and pleated with some ugly brown shoes and you are good to go!

Have some fun with your dress code. Clothe yourself as ridiculously as possible while still remaining within the confines of the code. Collared shirt required? Why not find one that extends about a foot in each direction? Have to wear a belt? Get a buckle the size of a license plate that has a big middle finger engraved on the front. Skirt has to extend below the knees? Droop it until it does.

Ties

The main purpose of clothing is to provide warmth and protection, so based on that, let's analyze some clothing types:

Pants: covers legs, ass, and junk

Analysis: useful

Shirt: covers upper body, including the sensitive nipple region

Analysis: useful

Tie: - a portion of it strangles your neck while the rest hangs limp and creates a paper shredder hazard

Analysis: USELESS!

Despite its uselessness, a tie is considered professional attire. Why exactly? For the little dash of color? If that's the case, then it shouldn't matter if I tie the damn thing around my head.

I have seen grocery stores that require their grocery baggers and shelf stockers to wear white shirts and ties. Newsflash: They're not lawyers, they're store clerks! The store's attempt to make their employees look more professional only becomes more of an insult. Not only are they bagging people's toilet paper for minimum wage but they are forced to feel strangulated by fashion gingerbread while doing so. If ever an employee deserved to wear jeans, this would be the time.

Ironing

I consider ironing to be one of the biggest time-wasters next to making the bed. If you desire to enter the workplace wrinkle-free, then it is evident you still give a shit. There is freedom in wrinkled clothing. You never have to iron again. There's ten more minutes of sleep right there. Wrinkles send a message to those around you. They say, "Ironing is for pussies. I have better things to do." Your boss may mistake them for wrinkles caused by hard work. The opposite sex sees a person who, in the heat of passion, will rip their clothes off and let them fall where they may. Who wants someone who is going to ruin the moment by taking the time to neatly fold their clothing as they remove it?

Name Tags

My feelings are mixed on the use of name tags. On the one hand, name tags make it difficult to remain anonymous. It’s much easier for customers and coworkers alike to submit complaints about you if they know your name. On the other hand, they can be rather handy for a person like myself, who can't remember names for shit. One quick glance at the tag and you're saved from feeling like an ass for not remembering the name of the person you've been working with for two years.

Name tags are a favorite place for employers to display to the public how long you've worked for them. This can work for you or against you. If your name tag displays that you've been there for ten years, people will expect you to know what you're doing. If you've recently started and you get one of those, "Hi, I'm new and I'm learning" name tags, hang on to that sucker. It gives you license to be a total fuck up. "Kim, you've been here for three years, I think it’s time for a new name tag."

"No way! I'm still learning!"

Facial Hair

Employers need to lay off facial hair restrictions, even if it means some workers will grow one of those giant beards that can support its own ecosystem. Men (and occasionally women) sometimes feel the need to grow a beard. This is especially true if you hate your job. What? How do you make that connection? Well, like this: Growing facial hair is one of the few things you have control over in life if you aren't wealthy and in charge of your own time. That would apply to most of us. You might think, I hate my spouse, my kids are stupid, prescription-drug-addicted monkeys, and I hate my job, but at least I can grow a fucking beard!

Chapter 8

Getting to Work

"Anyone who can walk to the welfare office can walk to work."

-Al Capp

What if the welfare office is a lot closer?

Snow

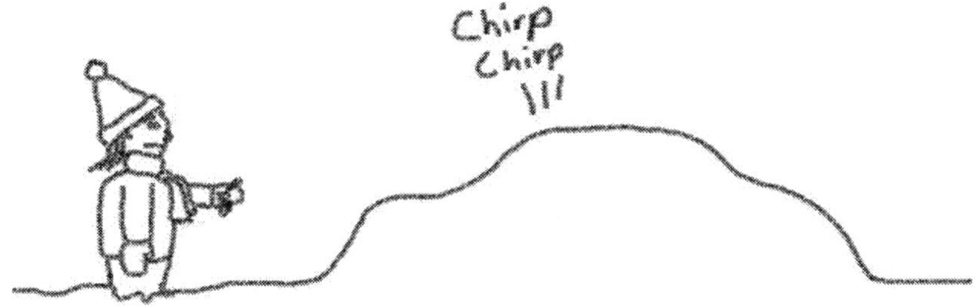

Some people may think snow is pretty, but these people probably have winter homes near the equator. For the schmoe trying to get to his job, it is anything but pretty. Snow is the world's way of taking a white, fluffy, frozen piss on the worker.

Get a remote starter for your car, even if you have to turn tricks, sell organs, or steal from your mother-in-law to pay for it. It's one of the greatest investments a cold-weather schmoe can make. With the push of a button from indoors, you'll have a warm defrosted car waiting for you while your neighbor chisels away and swears at the iceberg in the driveway.

Doing donuts in your work parking lot helps to ease the winter blues. Remember, losing control is all part of the fun so damaging company property is worth extra points. If your boss gives you any shit, just let her know that you temporarily lost control of your vehicle due to the unsafe conditions of their parking lot and are considering a lawsuit. And if you were planning to quit soon anyway, hit her in the face with a pee-soaked snowball.

The Commute

As if being at work isn't bad enough, we actually have to spend time getting there. Whether it's a five minute jaunt or a life-wasting hour long commute, in a nice SUV or on a crappy bicycle, one thing is common among schmoes: it sucks. The psychological torment of work anticipation is enough to cause weeping, vomiting, diarrhea, or all three at once.

Ways to Cope With the Commute

Fantasies - One way to cope with the commute is to fantasize. One of my personal favorites is to imagine I'm in a James Bond type car, and I have machine guns and missiles to blow away all the bastards that piss me off. I imagine evading capture from the police with strategic use of my trick license plate, smoke screen, oil slick, road spikes, and other super-awesome spy shit. I suppose one must be careful how much they indulge in such fantasies as they could probably lead to actual highway shootings.

Music - Listening to music is a great way to get yourself all pumped up and feeling good. Eventually, however, you get to work. Then it's like letting all the air out of a balloon, fart sound and all.

Media - Things like books, newspapers, crossword puzzles, movies, and the internet are some other distractions while you are driving to help you forget you're going to work. Unfortunately, they might also make you forget that you're driving. I'm willing to bet that accidentally killing someone is worse than working.

Masturbation - Self pleasure while driving is a special form of multitasking that is best left to the professionals, or the extremely horny that might wreck if they DON'T touch themselves.

The Slow Poke

When you're trying to get to work, there always seems to be at least one asshole in front of you who apparently has nowhere to be. Who are these fuckers that decide 7AM is a great time for a leisurely drive? Not once have I thought, "I love watching the sunrise through my car window with a line of angry traffic backed up behind me."

Oftentimes you recognize the same slowpoke on a regular basis. Identification of the perpetrator is the first step in enacting your plot for revenge. One day, get in front of him. If he likes to drive 20, go 10. Occasionally stop for no reason. Put on your turn signals randomly. Sit at an intersection all the way through the green light until it turns red again. If he ever tries to pass, swerve to block him. If you already drive a shitty car, slam on the brakes so he rear ends you, then calmly keep driving.

Another plan is to follow him until he stops somewhere. When he leaves his car, plant some contraband in the trunk, like drugs, weapons, body parts, etc. Then all it takes is one anonymous phone call to the authorities and voila! Mr. Slow Poke is going to the pokey to get a good poking.

The Passing Lane

There is a disturbing number of people that do not understand the function of the passing lane. The passing lane is not a place to hang out, sight see, daydream, jerk off, or go a fraction of a mile per hour faster than the semi on your right. The passing lane is for ... drum roll ... passing! Imagine that! Pass the car in the right lane quickly and move the fuck over. A concept so simple, it's right in the name!

I recommend using an air horn to get around these fuckers. Forget flashing your lights and using your factory horn. People aren't in any hurry to get out of the way of a meeping strobe light. Blast that air horn, however, and they'll be shitting bricks when they think they're about to get run over by a train. You can also scare the crap out of people on the sidewalk just for the fun of it. Just try not to give any old people a heart attack, unless they're retired upper management.

If you manage to get around one of these left lane lollygags, be sure to give them the finger. If it happens to them enough times, maybe they'll actually figure out why they're getting the finger.

Riding the Bus

Unless you're a thrifty big city dweller, riding the bus to work probably means you're a bit down on your luck. You've either lost your license, can't afford a car, or don't even know how to drive one. Whatever the case may be, riding the bus is not boosting your self-esteem.

On the bright side, you get to meet all sorts of interesting people on the bus. You get to spend time with society's marginal characters that you would not otherwise interact with. They each have a unique story and body odor to share, and often you needn't even ask them to share because they're already telling it out loud to themselves. Be nice, their lives may actually suck more than ours.

Carpooling

Even though carpooling may save money at the pump, the price is still paid in many other ways. For starters, you have entered into a relationship with people in which the only things you might have in common are geography and your workplace. This amounts to either awkward silence, really annoying conversation, or both. "No Megan, I can't guess what your cat did this morning, but I can't wait to hear about it."

Secondly, there's always one person who struggles with being ready on time. Inevitably you sit in their driveway for ten minutes honking while they give you the "just a minute" finger, standing there with no pants on and a toothbrush hanging out of their mouth. Apparently they do not care if they get fired, nor the rest of you in the car as well.

Another problem is that carpooling rarely works out fairly. Either someone doesn't drive their share, doesn't have enough gas money, lives in a highly inconvenient location, etc. The car pool is a great way for the mooch to work his magic.

Carpooling also means you are stuck at work for the duration. Never mind if you get diarrhea, too bad if Ned has to work an extra hour 'cause he fucked something up, you're stuck there until everyone's ready to go home. Even without any mayhem, it still takes longer to get to work and longer to get home. I'm no mathematician, but I'm pretty sure that adds up to even less free time.

Speeding Tickets

A speeding ticket has the ability to fuck up your work day even before it has begun. On top of being late, your labor now goes to pay a fine. There's nothing like the feeling of pissing your money straight down the drain, right into the shit-stained hands of the government. The police are supposed to serve and protect, but it seems another of their specialties is to harass and annoy the schmoe as they extract revenue for the government.

Supposedly ticketing speeders is in the interest of public safety. Why is it then when they pull someone over they create a far more dangerous situation than the speeding ever did? They force you to park on the shoulder, sometimes even jutting into a lane of travel while vehicles come whizzing by. How many videos have you seen of cops and their victims getting smashed to shit on the side of the road? These were all tragedies that could have been avoided by not pulling them over in the first place. Leave us speeders alone. We're in a hurry because we have more important things to do than get smeared on the shoulder.

Funeral Procession

As if the drive to work isn't depressing enough, it can be made worse by getting stuck behind a funeral procession. Now not only are you trying to cope with getting through your day, you're made late by a long, slow reminder of your mortality. Death sucks, but I'm not sure why it necessitates fucking up traffic. You know you really hate your job when your foremost thought about the person in the hearse is, "At least they don't have to go to work."

The Parking Lot

The parking lot is a place of danger, mystery, fierce competition, jealous rivalries, and in most cases, asphalt.

If you work for a large company, that means large parking lots which translate to a long ass run to the time clock. You may have gotten to the premises on time, but because of earlier shifts, annoying go-getters, and inconvenient landscaping you still end up late because you had to park on the outer rings of Saturn.

If you work at a place with customers, you get screwed on many levels. The customers get preferential parking over the employees, so once again your parking location sucks. Customers drive and walk like maniacs, especially when they come in the form of old people or children. Neither of these age demographics have high survival potential in the chaos of a parking lot. They also enjoy discarding random things in the parking lot, so when on foot you find yourself dodging things like fresh chewing gum, lugeys, used syringes and dirty diapers. I generally don't like rain, but at least the piles of puke get washed away.

Dog Poop

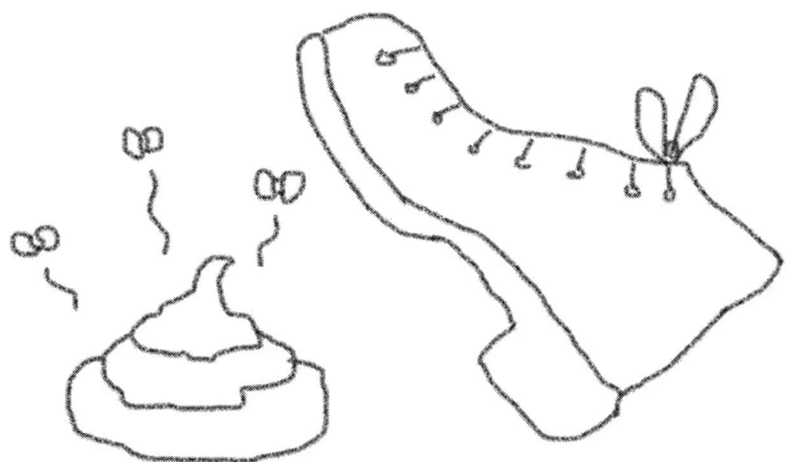

There are many ways to start your day off on the wrong foot, and stepping in doggie doo is literally one of them. If you started walking with the opposite foot, you probably would have missed it. But instead, you feel the nice soft squish of your shoe compressing the turd, forcing the soft nougat to squeeze its way between the tread. The experience can be all the more gratifying if you don't even have a dog.

But it could be worse. There are those times that you don't notice that you've stepped in it. At least not until it's too late to change your shoes. You have that pleasant mystery poop smell following you around for a while. Maybe you think one of your coworkers crapped himself. You might continually make remarks about how something really stinks, oblivious to the fact that it's coming from you. When you finally do figure it out you feel like quite the dumb ass, especially as you stand over the sink washing the bottom of your shoe.

Security Guards

Some offices have big, fat, friendly guys or old guys on stools with wheels at the entrance. They refer to these dudes as security guards, although when one is present I rarely feel more secure. I'm not exactly sure how a fat, lazy guy sitting in a chair all day is making the perimeter more secure. A perimeter he, himself, can't physically walk around, by the way.

I can't knock security guards for doing what they do, however. If a company is willing to pay them to sit on their asses and do nothing, more power to them. Take the fucking job. But sitting on your ass all day isn't as easy as it looks. Have you ever tried to sit on your butt for eight hours with nothing to do? It's virtually impossible to stay awake. All the blow in the world isn't enough to keep you from passing out.

Occasionally you get the ex-cop type of guards that take their jobs very seriously. These guys don't fuck around if you don't have your badge. After a lengthy strip search the guard will take some DNA and only when your identity has been verified, will you gain entrance into your place of employment. Just one more pain in the ass you have to deal with in a place you don't want to be in to begin with (especially if you get a cavity search).

Chapter 9
Rules, Signs, and Stuff

"If I'd observed all the rules, I never had got anywhere."
- Marilyn Monroe
We thank her for her disobedience. Bad girl.

Policies

Every company has their own special rules and policies. These were made up by someone higher up the ladder, and in most cases accomplish nothing but justification of that person's job. We all know down on the ground level that most of the policies are nothing short of retarded. Too often they complicate rather than simplify things, and almost always add some form of paperwork. This is especially true in government jobs. The government is adept at creating pointless paperwork. In fact, I think there are jobs dedicated to complicating things. They have bosses that look over their shoulders and say, "Nope, this process is still too easy. Create more forms to fill out."

Employee Handbooks

If your company needs a handbook to keep track of all their rules, then they have too many rules! Do you really need more than a simple few? I think don't be an asshole, show up, and do your job covers most of the bases. Most people can handle that if you leave them alone. If you write an entire book full of crap that treats people like children, don't be surprised when they act like children.

Weapons in the Workplace

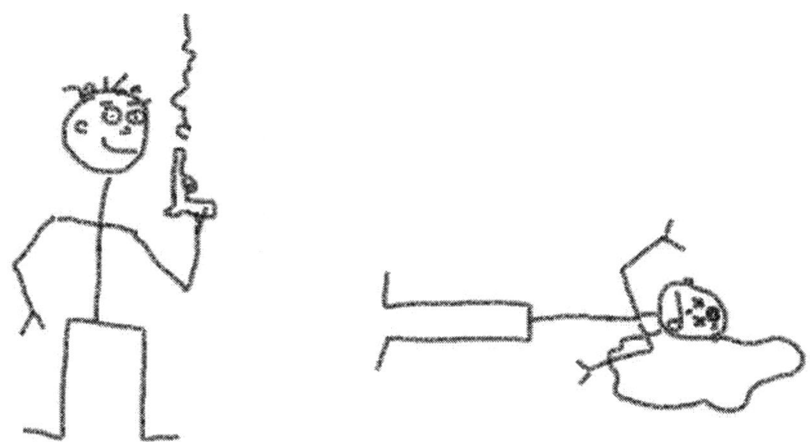

It is a common policy to strictly prohibit guns and other weapons in the workplace. This policy, while perhaps well-intentioned, is about as ass-backwards as reasoning can get. The main accomplishment of this prohibition is the disarmament of the people that can help you in the event that someone goes bananas. When a disgruntled employee decides he wants to come to work and kill everyone, do you think he's going to pay any attention to the weapons ban? Now, thanks to the weapons prohibition, the only person armed is the crazy motherfucker killing everyone.

No Food or Drink

Well this just plain sucks. Work makes me hungry. Work makes me thirsty. Food and drink are what keep me alive and give me the energy to do work in the first place. Management cannot truly be interested in efficiency when they're not letting their employees maintain a comfortable blood sugar level.

I suppose it could be dangerous to have consumables around the equipment. This is a problem easily solved with beer helmets. Another issue for some employers is that they feel it doesn't look professional around customers. I think it's probably more unprofessional when an employee passes out and bonks their head off the counter.

Chewing gum is another problem. They often don't want you to chew gum, but how can you get good service from someone that you can't even get close to because their breath smells like old butt cheese?

Music

Music in the workplace is often forbidden. It is considered unprofessional, distracting, and detrimental to productivity. What they often fail to realize is that without such distractions, the worker can become acutely aware of the suck factor of her job. The more you hate what you're doing, the more your body and mind resist the activity. Therefore, in their attempt to increase productivity by forbidding music, they have succeeded in destroying it further. Good job, upper management!

At the very least they should allow country music, because it's written for the worker. Just about every song is about working hard for money but coming up short, then sucking it up to get back out there and do it again. That can create a mindset for the schmoe and an image they want to attain. "I want to get up and work at my crappy low paying job and not take any time off because I'm tough and my family depends on me!" If you find yourself feeling that way, that's alright, it will make you more productive and a better worker. Just stay away from rap. You'll want hoes, mansions, nice cars, and no job. Actually....that sounds pretty good yo!

Practical Signs and Posters

Many signs and posters are meant to provide useful, simple, and practical information, but they often fail in serving their purpose. Sometimes I'll see a sign for a business, usually a bar, that says, "Open from 10am to close." That sign is half useless. What time do they open? It says 10am, okay that is useful. Now what time do they close? Closing time. Well no shit! I always assume places stay open until they close, don't you? Now maybe they don't have a set closing time each night, but give me a ball park at least! If I came in at 11pm will I find wine, women, and song or a locked door? They might as well put on their sign, "Closed until 10am."

Inspirational Posters

Some posters try to motivate, inspire, or improve your attitude. They might have a nature photo with a word and a quote, or some other kind of bullshit that attempts to uplift. You only see this kind of poster in office environments. If you tried to hang one up at a construction site I'm pretty sure you'd get the piss beat out of you by a mustached man in a hard hat.

Why would someone need inspiration and a positive lift at work? Sounds like someone out there already knows your job sucks, doesn't it? You might actually see one that does inspire you but that is short-lived until the next event that pisses you off. On average that event is about 8 minutes later, according to statistics we just made up.

Employees Must Wash Hands

EMPLOYEES MUST WASH
HANDS, FEET, MOUTH,
KNEES, ELBOWS, CHEST,
ASS, AND CROTCH
BEFORE RETURNING TO
WORK.
THANK YOU,
BROTHEL MGMT.

Workplace restrooms often have signs that say "Employees Must Wash Hands Before Returning to Work." The main goal of this sign is to give customers the illusion that the employees have clean hands. In reality, the chef may be cooking a little e-coli into your meal. If you're the type of person that doesn't wash your hands after using the bathroom, a sign isn't going to convince you to do so.

Furthermore, many signs have a technicality in their wording.

It tells them to wash "hands" but it does not specify whose hands. They only require that hands in general be washed. In that case, I want to wash Chloe's hands, and the rest of her for that matter. Or perhaps I will bring my extensive collection of rubber hands to work and give them a good scrubbing. Also, isn't this sign prejudicial to the handless employees? It doesn't make any references to hooks or other prosthetics. Maybe it's easier to keep them clean after a good deuce. I don't know.

Bulletin Boards

Bulletin boards in the workplace serve as a central location where information can be posted that no one will read. You can usually find out what is on the board by screwing something up and getting reprimanded for not reading it.

Or there are the boards where employees can post messages like "free kittens." This board is generally read more often as it can be a great form of entertainment and a good place to pick up a pee-stained mattress nice and cheap.

Bulletin Board Pranks

Whichever type of bulletin boards you find in your workplace, they are an excellent opportunity to have a little fun and screw with people. Here are some ideas for fake bulletins you can post at work:

- Puppies available for delicious meat and soft pelts
- Donut consumption no longer permitted
- Party at manager's house tonight, feel free to bring shady friends and illicit drugs
- When ladies room is occupied, women may use the sinks in the men's room
- Starting this week! Topless Tuesdays and Fornication Fridays!
- If you see trash on the floor, help them up
- What's ours is yours, please take supplies home
- Smelly farts are strictly prohibited
- For good weed, see Bob
- Orgy Planning Committee's next meeting is Tuesday, 7pm at Dale's house

Chapter 10

Job Safety

"Be regular and orderly in your life, so that you may be violent and original in your work."

- Gustave Flaubert

Until someone gets hurt and then you get fired.

Safety First

"Safety first" was not a phrase used before lawyers became ambulance chasers. Now every company preaches safety at every turn. You have to watch videos, sit through meetings, and sign paperwork that says you understand the videos and safety meetings. So does that mean the company really cares about you? Fuck no! It's to keep the lawyers away. Isn't that a great place to be? You are stuck between a company that wants to SEEM like it cares and bloodsucking lawyers who want to win money and see that no one would ever want to hire you again. Better hope that settlement is enough to live on.

Blood in the Workplace

Blood didn't used to be such a big deal. So you're bleeding from the ears a little bit? Suck it up! Wipe it off your work area with your shirt and get back to it! Nowadays, if you work in an overly cautious workplace, you cut your pinky finger and there are accident reports, blood cleanup protocol, release forms, investigations... No one wants to be sued and we have to assume that everyone might have AIDS. Stupid AIDS ruined sex, hardcore drugs, and workplace injuries.

First Aid Kits

A first aid kit is a very useful tool to have available in a workplace. That is, of course, if the kit is properly maintained. All too often the kit is an afterthought rather than a priority. In these cases, you are more likely to catch infection from the kit rather than prevent it. These kits can usually be identified by the rusty door with bloody fingerprints. If you see that, this box should be your last aid, not your first. There's nothing waiting for you in that dirty box but tetanus and tuberculosis.

Evacuation plans

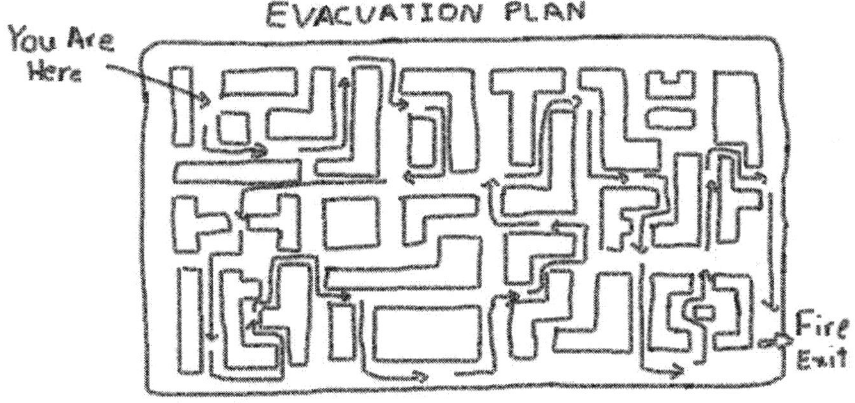

As a matter of safety (and potential law suits), every workplace has an evacuation plan. Your area will have a designated route to exit and a place to meet outside the building. This is all in case the place catches fire or some other emergency occurs. They always want to keep it orderly even though everyone's instinct is to run like a motherfucker! If you're fat and work on a high floor, you might weigh your options about burning versus hitting all those stairs. The bottom line is that if you know it's not a drill and danger is at your back, the nice, neat, and orderly evacuation plan is out the window. In fact for some people the window IS the evacuation plan.

Hazardous Substances

Some companies take hazardous material safety to the extreme. In these cases you practically have to suit up in HAZMAT gear to clean up spilled milk. It's nice that you don't have to be exposed to toxic chemicals, but the price is paid in paperwork, procedures, and the like. On the other hand, some companies just don't give a shit. They act like cancer and black lung are part of the retirement plan. Often the workers don't help the case, treating you like a big pussy if you put in earplugs or wear a respirator. Maybe Steve doesn't care, but I'm not really interested in going deaf and dying at age forty for twelve bucks an hour. It's tough for the schmoe. If you're not willing to eat lead paint chips for eight hours a day, there are ten people lined up behind you who will because they need the money.

Equipment

Most jobs require some type of equipment. Unfortunately, in an effort to keep expenses down, employers often neglect to keep their equipment up to snuff. They seem unable to factor in the cost of repairs and lost productivity while they're "saving money." Of course whether you're working with brand new, state of the art goods or some old broken down piece of crap, you'll still be expected to get the work done. “Carol, did you get all the informational packets finished yet?"

"Nope, I spent the last hour and a half trying to fix this five dollar stapler."

Chapter 11
Bosses

"Hard work spotlights the character of people: some turn up their sleeves, some turn up their noses, and some don't turn up at all."

- Sam Ewing

And some turn up just when you don't want them to because they get paid to tell YOU to work hard.

Boss Commercial

"If you aren't satisfied with your career, then ask yourself the following: Do you jump to conclusions without having all the facts? Do you accuse people of things without knowing the whole situation? Would you like to make a large income while having to do little?"

"If you answered 'Yes' to any of these questions then you might have what it takes to be upper management! Why bother toiling away in a dead end job when you can be dangerously unqualified and tell people what to do? Don't wait another miserable day. Call now!"

Superiors

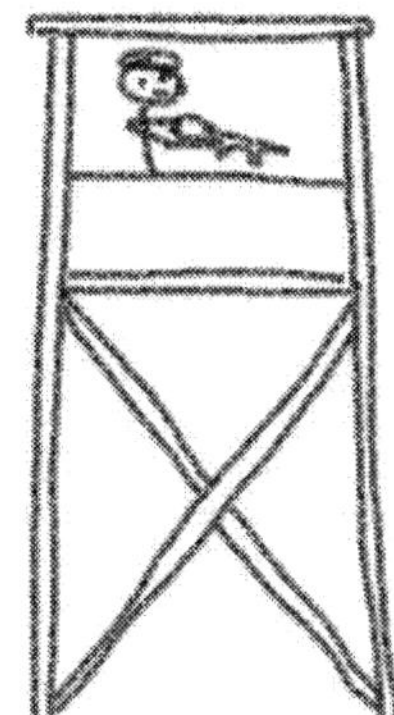

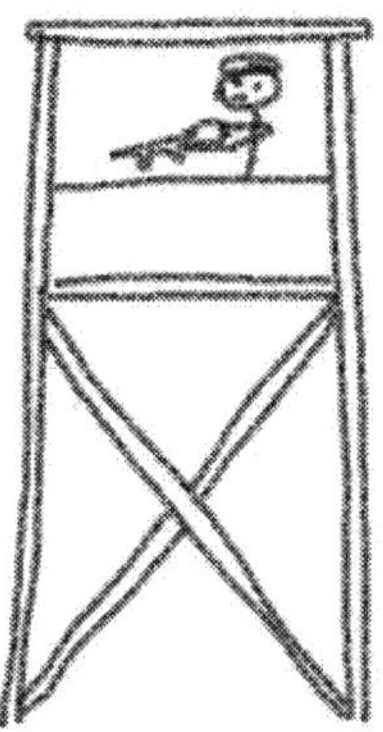

Don't you just love the term "superiors"? I just picture the bosses two stories up, watching us all work below, while they're pacing back and forth, wielding machine guns.

Other than being higher in job ranking, how often is a boss really superior? It seems the schmoe is usually wondering how such a dipshit ended up in that position. Did they know someone, was HR feeling lazy, or did they give head to get ahead?

Mini Bosses

Sometimes your boss isn't the one telling you what to do. You might have a coworker who takes it upon themselves to tell you what to do. A diet or mini boss is what I like to call them. The one difference between the two...mini bosses have no actual power. Yes, they can dish out commands but you don't have to listen or follow through. This is where you can have some fun with people like that. Tell them, "Okay, I'll get right on that." Then do nothing.

I think they like to show that they CAN be in charge if they were just given the chance. What they don't know is that the boss usually finds them annoying and ass-kissy. So really the joke is on them. The people they boss around don't listen and the boss doesn't like them. There is such balance in nature.

Unnecessary Bosses

In every business operation, there is at least one boss whose responsibilities are a mystery. No one can figure out exactly what they are supposed to be doing and why their job is necessary. These bosses must know this, so they occasionally do things to try to justify their jobs and make it look like they actually work. They will occasionally send out memos or post things on the bulletin board. They will also require you to "run things by them" so they can give you their "OK" as if their opinion was in some way useful and necessary. They don't want people to realize that everything would function just fine if they were removed from the equation.

Unnecessary bosses are like ties. For some reason, the company feels you need them even though they cost money, don't do anything, and you can easily do your job without them. In fact, they usually get in the way, and make you uncomfortable. Ties are useful for one thing: strangling useless bosses.

Performance Reviews

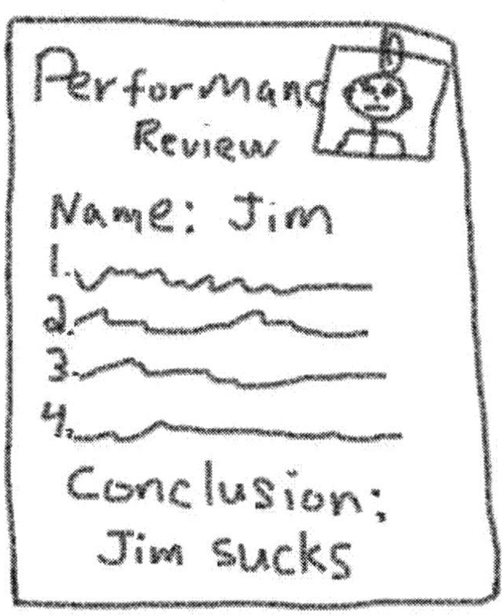

Everyone has to go through a performance review at some point during the year. This is when your boss can tell you why you are a model employee or why you suck. Even if you feel you are a good employee, you can usually expect to get some criticism. "Well Jim, you show up on time, you get your work done quickly and accurately. From what I can see looks great." Jim starts to get up and walk out when..."Ahh, there's just one small little thing, if I had to pick something that you might want to work on. Your deodorant could use a switch. What is that shit anyway? Whoo! I think I'd rather smell your BO there, Jim. Take care and keep up the good work!"

Deadlines

Deadlines can be motivators for the procrastinators who otherwise get nothing done. To me deadlines are more like instigators. Having someone barking at me to get something done by a certain time just pisses me off. Get off my back and I'll get it done when I get it done. Am I suddenly getting paid more for working faster? Not likely. What is so important that needs done so fast? Okay, maybe something like getting an adrenaline shot for someone in anaphylactic shock, but not much else.

Caught by the Boss

Everyone has a moment or two where you slack a little or cut a corner. You're only human! What your boss says to you in these times can be funny. Maybe you're clowning around and you see your boss standing there with her mouth gaping open. She'll usually say something like, "I did NOT just see you do that!" To which you can reply, "GOOD! Because I'm not supposed to be doing that!"

Suspension

If you've been written up too many times you could get a suspension. Sound like high school to anyone? Suspensions crack me up. How is staying home punishment? The reason you got in trouble in the first place is because you hate going to work. If they really wanted to punish you, they should make you work all kinds of overtime. Instead for your bad behavior you get to sleep in and watch TV. What's next? "Johnson, I'm warning you, one more offense and we're sending you and your family on a tropical vacation!"

Bosses Statements and the Schmoe's Secret Answers

A boss, like a parent, can say a lot of stupid things to you. Luckily, you have the things that you say to yourself under your breath to keep you from getting too angry.

Boss: "How many times do I have to tell you?"
Schmoe: "Six. Yeah I think six would do it."

Boss: "Tell me why I shouldn't fire you."
Schmoe: "I need money."

Boss: "Can't you work any faster?"
Schmoe: "I can, but working slowly is easier."

Boss: "You're doing it wrong."
Schmoe: "I know. I'm hoping if I keep doing it wrong you don't make me do it anymore."

Boss: "Tuck in your shirt."
Schmoe: "You see it as my shirt not tucked into my pants. I see it as my pants being tucked into my shirt."

10 Things to Yell at Your Boss Within Earshot of Coworkers When You Get Fired

1. You're firing me because I found out you're gay?

2. Wow, so I'm just the first of many firings? Good luck with that.

3. I promise I'll never tell the police where the body is!

4. Really? I had no clue you kept blow in your middle left drawer. Huh!

5. Hey and thanks again for all the secret raises.

6. So we didn't get raises because of your five figure bonus?

7. What? You'll think about giving my job back if I give you everything in my wallet?

8. You're right, the only thing we ever agreed on was that Fred is a douche.

9. My job has been outsourced to your trousers? What is that supposed to mean?

10. Yeah just lay low another 5 years until she's 18, then go public with it.

Chapter 12

Scheduling

"Work expands so as to fill the time available for its completion."

- C. Northcoat Parkinson

No sense rushing when you get paid by the hour.

On Call

Putting someone on call is an employer's way of treating them like a booty call. They won't commit to giving you a full day's work and pay, but they don't want you to be doing anything else either. They only want you if they need you, and if they need you, you better be there.

This arrangement makes sense in some situations. An ER doctor, for example, might rather be chillin' at home instead of the hospital when there is only the possibility of an emergency. Doctors are generally paid well and know this comes with the territory when they start the job. However, on call status makes far less sense when you work somewhere like a video store. Yes, ladies and gentlemen, video stores will put employees on call, as if someone's life may depend on the timely rental of a new release. Give them the shift or don't give them the shift, but don't fuck with their lives over minimum wage.

If you find yourself in this unfortunate situation, have a little fun with it. When they call you in, burst through the front door completely naked, soaking wet, with a head full of shampoo. As you catch your breath yell, "I got here as fast as I could! Where's the entertainment emergency?

Swing Shifts

The word swing almost tricks you into thinking it's something fun. Whether you're talking about a playground, music, or a special party for open-minded adults, swing usually means a good time. Not in the case of work. Swing shifts are an employer's way of destroying your sleep schedule and shortening your lifespan so they may produce around the clock. They smash your circadian clock with a hammer and replace it with their time clock. There is nothing like working when your body says you should be sleeping.

Those in charge of the scheduling the swing shifts normally work days. Isn't that convenient? It seems those in control of our misery rarely have to experience it for themselves. If you have such a scheduler, and they show little consideration for your quality of life, have some fun with theirs. Pass the time on your midnight shift by repeatedly prank calling them. On your lunch break, take a ride to their house and set off fireworks outside their bedroom window. Call the police, pose as a neighbor, and report a robbery in progress at their house. Do whatever you can think of to teach them a valuable lesson on the effects of sleep deprivation.

Job Sharing

At first thought, job sharing sounds like something nice. I think of cooperation and teamwork, "helping a brotha out," that sort of thing. Maybe you have to lift heavy stuff, so you say, "This shit is really heavy," and your boss says, "I'll have Bob give you a hand with that heavy shit." This would be an incorrect illustration of job sharing. In this world of better bottom lines, job sharing can be used as a way to get out of paying benefits by using part-time workers to do a full-time job. Instead of one person possibly making a living, you have two or more people with no health insurance who need second jobs. Why stop the cost cutting there? How about food sharing? Uniform sharing? Chair sharing? Maybe the part-timers can just move in together and share things like spouses, kids, beds, and bathwater.

Scheduled Naps

Companies would do well to include a nap break in the work day. How much work do you really get done after lunch? Most of the energy during that time is spent fighting to stay awake. A two hour nap after chow would solve that problem. You'd probably get more done in the last couple hours than you would have if you remained awake the whole time.

Job Rotation

Job rotation can be a good thing if you can't stand your current tasks and would like to try something new. However, it seems the schmoe rarely gets what he wants, so if you're eager for job rotation the best you'll probably get is a chair that spins. On the contrary, the schmoe may be forced to change jobs against his will. The employer says they want to stimulate and challenge their workers by cross-training them. What they really do is aggravate the shit out of them by pulling them out of a job they were comfortable with and making them do something that sucks even more. Here's an idea for job rotation: Let's stick the managers in the shittiest jobs and let the schmoes boss them around for a while. Who knows, everyone might just learn something.

Chapter 13

Psychological Effects of Work

"Nobody can think straight who does not work. Idleness warps the mind."

- Henry Ford

Oh yeah Henry? I think work can warp the mind too. Have you ever heard of disgruntled employees going crazy? I never hear of disgruntled lazy people. They might be but they aren't going to do anything about it!

Positive Attitude

We had a meeting at work once about creating a positive attitude in the workplace. Most of us thought, "This is going to suck." Not a good start.

Death of individuality

Companies tend to try to diminish your personality in favor of a generic, corporate, company-wide persona. I've been to interviews where they don't even talk to you, they just hand you a test to see if you have the correct personality type to fit their plan (AKA, able to be brainwashed and bow in submission at their whim). If your test comes back with the results that you are a person who has a strong personality and is confident in themselves, right out the door you go.

Take working in a call center for example. They give you a script of exactly what to say to people who call in. Why? Because you can't be trusted to speak on your own! Shut up, answer the phone, read the script, get the call completed in certain time frame, and take the next call! To be fair, companies have to do that because, let's face it, there are a lot of idiots out there. That's why when you call an 800 number it sounds like you are talking to a robot, many times a robot in India named Skip.

We have sacrificed that personal touch of the individual for the broad, monotone, company blah of the script. It's not even a good script at that! “My goal was to provide you with excellent customer service, did I do that today?” No one talks like that! That seems like something a hostage would say to a camera. “Please say yes, I can confirm that the company has all the means necessary to launch a full scale firing of my ass.”

Working With Depression and Anxiety

If you have a job you don't like, you are inevitably working with depression and anxiety. I suppose all that varies from person to person is the degree. People might ask what's wrong or tell you to cheer up and smile. "What's wrong? Nothing much, just trying not to throw myself out the window as I wonder how my life turned out like this. But you know what would make me smile? Punching you in the face!"

Wouldn't it be nice to get financially reimbursed for this kind of misery? Why does workman's comp generally pay for physical injuries but not mental ones? If work helped break your brain, shouldn't work pay damages? “So, why do you feel you deserve workman's compensation?”

“I used to be a happy, well-adjusted person before I started working. Now I have several diagnosable psychological conditions. You do the math.”

Try to Sound Happy (A smile in your voice)

I have worked in call centers more times than I care to mention. Once I had a boss that said that we should have a smile in our voices when we talk to people. She said if we have trouble doing this, try to think of something that makes you happy right before you answer the phone. This was her technique!

So, being a man in my early twenties, I went right to sex. The problem with that is that my voice didn’t sound happy, so to speak, but turned on. “Oh so you are asking about your 401k? You want to know how big it is and how much it has grown?

Mmm, daddy likes that."

Years later, when my sex drive dwindled a half percent, I would think about quitting that very job to get to the same mindset. "Yeah, I would like to start drawing my pension."

"I bet you would you lazy piece of shit, what are you 48? A little early for retirement aren't we? Rich mommy and daddy? Huh?"

Work Environment

The vast majority of us work for companies that subscribe to the rigid, bright, sterile, and professional surroundings where seriousness reigns supreme. Anything beyond their flourescent paradise would be deemed a distraction. How that helps productivity and prevents worker burnout is beyond me.

About one percent of the companies do understand the benefit of a fun environment. They have low turn-over rates and happier workers. The employees do a better job and become more efficient. Unfortunately, you couldn't get into those companies if you were fucking the CEO. They get overloaded with resumes. Hmmm, funny that people would want to work at a place like that.

Work Weather

If the weather is perfect outside and you work indoors, you are bound to hear, "It's too nice outside to work in here today." On the other hand if the weather sucks you'll hear, "Man, the weather is too nasty to be in here today. I just want to go home and nap." Is there any weather that is perfect for working? Let me answer that for you, No!

Working Angry

Anger can hinder or help you in the workplace, depending on its degree of severity and how you use it. If you've literally killed your boss and coworkers with a machete and eaten some of their body parts, your anger has probably gotten a little out of hand and surpassed any usefulness. But if you harness the negative energy, you can channel it to help yourself. It might give you the balls to finally ask out the dreamboat from accounts payable. It might give you a different perspective on your work and show you sweet ways to cut corners and get rid of unnecessary bullshit to make your life easier. Or you might finally muster the stones to quit altogether to write books about crap jobs.

The Zone

A rare phenomenon can occur in which you are so focused on working that you temporarily forget about time and how much your job sucks. When you snap out of it, you realize that a nice chunk of time has passed and you are closer to being home. You actually feel sort of (gasp) happy. It is not known how this happens. Perhaps it's the alignment of the planets. Maybe it's some sort of temporary brain damage. It's like a blackout of sorts. Like when you're driving and you snap out of your reveries and don't remember driving. Or when you get totally shit-faced and you wake up in a strange place and have no idea where you are. It is a rare, temporary respite from the pain of working that must be cherished.

Multitasking

Unfortunately in today's work environments, doing one thing at a time is rarely enough. Employers want you to answer the phone, man the computer, wait on the customers, all the while with a smile on your face. Then they wonder why they get customer complaints and their employees make mistakes.

I feel multitasking sucks for a number of reasons. For one, I can't do it. For another, it's stressful. Still another, it degrades the quality with which you can complete each task. By doing several things at once you do several things shitty instead of one thing at least mediocre.

I'm always amazed when I go through a fast food drive thru and the worker is counting out my change while taking the next person's order. I think my head would explode. These people deserve more money and respect, not impatient jerks who want their dollar cheeseburgers right NOW!

Living in the Moment

Some people say they live in the moment. "Hey man, tomorrow might not come, and yesterday? That's dead and gone. I live for today, dude. I live for the here and now." You know who never says that? People who hate their jobs! How can you live in the moment if the moment sucks? I tend to project myself to a better place. I don't work the day shift, I work the day dreams.

So What Do You Do For a Living?

You get that question now and again. You might say you work in construction, as a mortgage loan officer, in retail, at a restaurant, etc. Those are all valid answers but we never mention what we REALLY do for a living. What do I do for a living? Well, I kill myself slowly with stress, hatred for my job, boiling internal rage, and then I take the edge off with alcohol, drugs, and stupid TV shows. That's what I do for a living, you?

10 Signs You Hate Your Job

1. You have a job.
2. Even though your mother died of lung cancer you take up smoking just for the breaks.
3. The words "I hate this job" are on continuous loop in your brain.
4. The jealousy you feel toward your pets when you leave for work is affecting your relationships with them.
5. You spend most of your day at work trying to avoid doing work.
6. You drink a lot of fluids just to get up and pee more.
7. You have your psychiatrist on speed dial.
8. You break down and cry in front of your drug dealer.
9. You start looking for rich 90-year-olds to marry ... and kill.
10. You write a book about how much work sucks.

Chapter 14
Chemical Assistance

"Work is the curse of the drinking classes."
-Oscar Wilde
Enough said.

Feeling Better

We medicate ourselves with drugs and alcohol to deal with the day-to-day monotony of work. In the long run it doesn't make us feel any better but it does in the moment. The stress we take home would be made better if we ate well and worked out but unfortunately that takes....effort. Yes, we burn less calories opening a beer bottle than running for 30 minutes but running doesn't get you drunk. There might be a runner's high but you have RUN to get there. There is also an after work lying on the couch high too, with chips and a cola of your choice.

Alcohol

Alcohol, also called "make me forget juice," is a staple for the schmoe. It's like a big liquid eraser that reboots the system. It helps to wash away any memories of the terrible week you had as well as any reminders that you're going to have to do it again next week.

The more wasted you get, the more effective the system re-boot. For example, a six-pack might help you forget about the frustration you have with your boss, whereas a case of beer might wash away the knowledge that you even have a boss or the meaning of the word frustration.

Beer, over many years of schmoedom, can cause what is known as the beer belly. Now many may view the beer belly as unhealthy, a form of obesity. That may be true to an extent, but it also indicates something else. It says, “I am a survivor. I get up day in and day out, and I go to work. And it sucks. It sucks balls. But did I give up? No! I kept going because I have kept drinking.”

Happy Hour

The work place can be stuffy, ripe with political correctness and a “don’t sue us” vibe. That’s why you need to cut loose and have some drinks with the people you work with. These are the people you go through it all with, the people who understand how it is. You want to go where everyone knows your name. If you wear a name tag, that would be anywhere, by the way.

Happy hour is a time to say and do shit that you would never do at work. You're out of the workplace jurisdiction and full of booze. Take off your tie, grab Brittany’s ass, and tell people how you really feel until you elicit the sarcastic response "Tell us how you REALLY feel."

Illegal Drugs

Let's face it, some jobs suck so bad that being in an altered state of consciousness is the only way to get through it. Before passing judgment upon people that choose to use drugs at work, let's remember, at least they are working. There are others that scam the system so they can sit at home to do their drugs in front of their giant televisions funded by tax payers.

Some people may not be comfortable knowing that the guy cooking their food just smoked a big fat joint before he started his shift. But these same people might not realize that being high may be the only thing stopping him from throwing the food in their face.

One worry about drugs in the workplace is that it will affect productivity. Apparently the policy makers are unfamiliar with the effects of cocaine and other uppers. Put a depressed sober woman next to one that's all hopped up on bump, and you tell me who's gonna work faster?

Prescription Drugs

Antidepressants, tranquilizers, and pain killers, oh my! If you are in mental, physical, or emotional pain, and you still have to go to work, these drugs are like a "keep your will to live" morning vitamin.

The use of these drugs has become more widespread because as a culture we're either becoming more acutely aware of the suck, or we're becoming bigger pussies, or both. Either way, the suck factor is there, and modern pharmacology is working hard to bring back our shit-eating grins.

One thing I find interesting about anti-depressants is that they come with the warning that they may increase the risk of suicidal thoughts and behavior. Why doesn't anyone warn you of the same risk when you start a shitty job?

Sleeping Pills

These little nuggets become necessary due to stress of the job, which creates insomnia, which makes the schmoe late for work, which gets the schmoe fired, which relieves job stress, which temporarily restores sleep, which makes the schmoe not want another job, which drains the savings, which causes the stress of having no money, which causes insomnia, which causes the schmoe to get another job ... rinse, repeat.

Addiction

Doctors and other professionals warn of drugs and alcohol being addictive. Well no shit. That's kind of a no-brainer. If something makes you feel better, there's a pretty good chance you're gonna do it again. You never hear warnings about the addiction potential of paperwork or floor mopping, and for good reason.

Caffeine

Since the schmoe is unlikely to experience energy from enthusiasm, caffeine is a staple used to get through the day. Whether from coffee, soda, energy drinks, or pills swallowed, snorted, injected, or sprinkled on our cereal, we get it however we can.

Some schmoes have the ability to survive solely on caffeine

and cigarettes at work. This seems to defy the laws of basic biology, but I suppose it's not that strange since working a shitty job defies every fiber of our being.

At some point you have to ask yourself, “Do I really want to be awake for this shit?” A happy medium between functionality and a haze might be the best option (see above regarding drugs).

Sugar

Sugar has always been my energy source of choice. People complain that it gives you energy for a short while, but then you crash. This is a problem easily solved by simply eating more sugar. There are always sweets in the office place. People bring in doughnuts and baked goods all the time. When those treats are combined with a sedentary job, people begin to complain about getting fat at work. Keep in mind that is what the arms on the chair are for: to act as a guide for your expanding ass. When snug, please refrain from eating any more sugary snacks.

Sugar or any food at work serves as another distraction. It's just one more thing to tweak out a tinge of joy. You hear of people who like their jobs so much they forget to eat. "I forgot to eat, HA! I was so focused on the task at hand, I just simply forgot to eat." The schmoe eats to forget, big difference.

Chapter 15

The Schmoe and Money

"Do not hire a man who does your work for money, but him who does it for love of it."

- Henry David Thoreau

Good luck finding that man! If you do, hurray! You can get away with paying him much less.

School

Of all the things you learn in school, practical life lessons are not on the list. You certainly learn how to diagram a sentence (something no one other than a teacher has done in their adult life) and ask permission to go to the bathroom (something to get used to when you get a job). However, most people don't learn how to balance a check book or be responsible with their money. This can mean being a slave to your debt, especially if you have loans for higher education, the schooling that ruins hobbies and usually provides little more than a minor schmoe upgrade.

If they really wanted to prepare us for the lifetime of work awaiting us, they need to change the curriculum. We need courses like "Dealing With an Asshole Boss 101," "The Importance of Drinking Regularly," and "How to Accept the Fact That You Might Not Be Special." When you are finished, you wouldn't graduate, you would be "let go".

Budgeting

Budgeting is an important yet also impossible task for the schmoe. It's important because there is a limited amount of financial resources that needs to be used wisely. It's impossible because there are so many unforeseen ways that the schmoe gets screwed that throw your budget into the toilet. Car problems, health problems, gas prices, layoffs, tornadoes, ice cream trucks, and the circus are just a few examples of forces that work against the schmoe being able to control spending and get ahead. Unless you've figured your way out of the proverbial rat race, it's best to keep some lube handy and just accept the fact that you'll be frequently taking it in the ass.

Extra Money

I've always been amazed at how low the pay is for most jobs. Sometimes I would look at my paycheck and think, if I spent 40 hours a week literally LOOKING for money I could find this much. That's one reason why there are so many homeless people walking around. They have figured that out already.

I understand it from the business point of view, but I often wonder what the company thinks people are actually doing with minimum wage. I have a feeling that the company believes that people are working for a concept such as "extra money." Listen, unless you are rich, there is no such thing as extra money! There is money and that's it. When you are a schmoe, every nickel is accounted for and needed. Perhaps their definition of a necessity is skewed and they consider food and shelter luxuries. I would like to see the bosses do a calculation and see if they could live on that pay. They might discover that unless people are single with roommates and a second job, their dental plan includes cheap whiskey and rusty pliers.

The Hourly Wage

The hourly wage places a monetary value on your life. If you make ten dollars an hour, it's another way of saying, "We think one hour of your living, breathing existence is worth $10.00. And we're buying it from you. It is no longer yours. We own you for that specified amount of time."

It's disheartening to know that your life can be worth so very little, so here are some ways to counterbalance low wages:

Slack off. If you waste company time, you actually make your value higher. Suppose each hour you only do fifteen minutes of work. If you were making ten dollars an hour, it's now like you make forty!

Steal. The more you take from the company, the more you increase your hourly worth. "You say I am worth ten dollars an hour? I say I am worth ten dollars, a stapler, and a roll of toilet paper, bitch!"

Get laid. Work can be a great place to meet people, socialize, and get some ass. The more you're able to line up dates during working hours, the less you'll feel bad about your sorry wages.

Do other work. Let's think of a totally random example here. Maybe you want to write a book about how much work sucks, and you need time to write it. Why not do it at the office on their equipment? It'll make you feel good that you're using their time and stuff to better your life.

Make your own schedule. Experiment and shake up your routine by busting your ass during your lunch period. Meanwhile, during the hours you're supposed to work go ahead and eat, make phone calls, and take care of personal business.

If any of these suggestions backfire and your boss threatens to fire you or call the authorities, just break down, cry, and tell him you were molested as a child. Once that is established, you should be able to keep your job and continue slacking.

Pay Periods

If you are a frugal, conservative, sober schmoe, it doesn't

really matter how often you get paid because you can make it last. Of course, you're probably not much fun either. If you're a spendthrift party schmoe, the scenario is quite different. For example, if this type of schmoe gets paid monthly, they and anyone near them probably has an amazing week or so. This is likely followed by a few weeks spent penniless, eating ramen noodles. If the party schmoe gets paid weekly, the amount of days spent noodle eating would only be a few days at a stretch, interspersed with smaller but more frequent substance abuse binges. I don't know of any scientific studies, but it seems clear to me there is a direct correlation between pay frequency and number of consecutive days a schmoe can stay fucked up.

Paying For Benefits

Most employers make you contribute part of your pay toward your benefits, and they still have the nerve to refer to them as "benefits." It's like having to buy your own birthday presents. If employers want to be shitty and not offer true benefits, that's their prerogative, but stop calling them benefits. Perhaps it takes up too much space in the classified ads to say "access to shitty company health plan with YOUR money" or "kind of like benefits if you assume a considerably lower wage than advertised."

Working on Commission

Commission jobs reach a new degree of suckitude because of the nature of the pay. At least with other jobs, at the end of a shitty day you know you're getting a paycheck. You can slave all day at a sales job and earn a big fat zero for your efforts.

If you are going to thrive at a commission job, you have to be highly motivated and have near-psychotic optimism. You also need to be gifted in the art of bullshit. I personally have none of these attributes. Unfortunately, I wasn't fully aware of how much I lacked them until after working a couple of commission jobs. Instead of convincing the customer to buy something, I more readily agreed with them that they didn't really need it. "Yeah, I wouldn't buy that piece of shit either. Now excuse me, I have to go be alone and hate my life."

Working For Tips

Working for tips is a humbling experience, as you get immediate feedback from strangers measured in dollars and cents. It's the monetary equivalent of being told "We liked you," or "You suck ass." Sometimes even when you gave the customer good service the money they left says, "Fuck you." I like to tip well even in the case of poor performance. I also like to tip people working jobs where it's not expected. I've worked service jobs, and I know how hard it can be just to show up, let alone plaster on a smile on top of your misery. You never know how hard that person's life might be. They might have been raped ... during their current shift. Their bad mood is unlikely anything personal unless, of course, you are being a complete asshole. I suppose it's your prerogative to be an inconsiderate dick face of a customer, but at least have the decency to be a tipping dick face.

A tip, by definition, is supposed to be a nice bonus for your service, but leave it to greedy business people to fuck that up. They either disallow the acceptance of tips, or they use the existence of tips as an opportunity to reduce wages and create dependence on the tips as regular income. Some employers will even take the tips from employees so they can be taxed, redistributed, or whatever else they might do with them. They want to have it both ways - to pay ultra shitty wages AND to treat your tips like THEIR money! I say, "Hands off assholes!" You're busting ass making them richer, and they want to fuck with money that might buy your dinner for the night. I hope these pricks get carpal tunnel so bad from counting their money that they can't feed THEMSELVES!

Taxes

As if the paltry wages of the schmoe weren't bad enough, on payday the government mafia steps in and takes what they feel is theirs. The government is like the bully at school that takes your lunch money. Somehow the bully feels he has a right to the money that you worked for. They take money from you and give it to people who have figured out that it's easier to sit at home and collect your money than it is to go to work and make their own.

Taxes should be avoided whenever possible. The government has far more money than it needs, they just don't know how to spend it. The government is like a teenage girl with daddy's credit card. By paying taxes, we are enablers. We continue to give them money to spend frivolously, and they don't learn their lesson. They just keep taking more and more money. We need to show them tough love. The kind of tough love you show to a compulsive gambler or a junkie. So I encourage you to not pay taxes whenever possible without going to jail in the process. Unfortunately, that's the tough part.

When the government has a budget deficit and they need more money, they can make it a law that you have to give them more. How is that fair? If the schmoe has a budget deficit, he can't walk into work and simply demand more money. The boss can just tell her to fuck off and she has to go back home to figure out what she can sell so her electric doesn't get shut off.

Status Symbols

People talk about nice cars as being status symbols. When you see someone driving a nice car you might think, "There is someone doing well for themselves. They probably have a good job, a nice house and boat." We forget that ANY car is a status symbol. When I swing my rustmobile with sagging ceiling upholstery and broken air conditioning into the parking lot, you know my status. You know things could be better and that I've probably made some mistakes. Either that or I'm some combination of dumb, lazy, and stoned. That's my status. Black people get screwed on the status symbol thing. If they are in a sweet ride, people won't just assume they are doing well. They might conclude they are drug dealers and/or the car is stolen. Sad but true.

10 Signs Your Job Doesn't Pay Enough

1. When you get your paycheck you owe THEM money.
2. You're always willing to give pyramid schemes a chance.
3. You make a list of what organs you could sell and still be alive.
4. When looking in the mirror, you wonder if someone would pay you for sex.
5. You start convincing yourself that being homeless is just like camping all the time.
6. The majority of dirt in your car consists of scratch off ticket shavings.
7. You start wondering how much your kids would be worth on the black market.
8. Keep wondering how long it's going to take for someone with money in your family to die.
9. You fantasize about getting hit by a well insured driver.
10. You pretend to work late but really live there because you can't afford rent.

Chapter 16
Work Characters

"Every group has its idiosyncrasies, but at a certain point we are all human."

- D.L. Hughley

And humans are goofy.

Coworkers

Every workplace has it's own special motley crew. However, there are certain types that seem to be present no matter where you work. Below, we've elaborated on just a few of the personalities you may run into at your place of employment.

The Overachiever

Description:
This person makes everyone else look bad due to their productivity and desire for advancement, securing ass beatings from coworkers.

Demeanor:
Mostly pleasant just as long as they are putting in longer hours.

Little Known Fact:
Somehow graduated with a 5.0 due to extra credit in high school.

How to Deal:
Have her do your work too. Compliment her on how efficient he is and how you'd like to see her do your work the same way. She'll be unable to resist, just be sure to take full credit for your recent improvement.

The Know It All

Description:
The Know-It-All can either be smart or totally stupid. If they are smart they may actually "know it all." If they are dumb, then they THINK they know it all but what they don't know, ironically, is that everyone knows they're dumb.

Experience:
Can be either a crusty old veteran of the job or the new guy who thinks his old company did things smarter and better.

Known For:
Taking over conversations
Jumping in to leadership roles
Annoying the piss out of coworkers

How to Deal:
The one thing you have over the Know-It-All is life experience. If you are in a group of people and the Know-It-All is spewing his "how to" knowledge, change the subject to partying or sex. Remember, while he was reading, you were fucking! Let him stumble in front of everyone to keep up.

The Smelly Guy

Description:
They are usually the larger of our species, but not always. Something they wear is usually stained with ...."something." If the sun hits them just right you can actually see a dim brown haze, in which they are encompassed.

Pros:
You can fart around him as much as you want and he won't notice. Even your worst fart will be absorbed into his thick cloud of funk.
If it's your boss he can never sneak up on you.

Cons:
He smells like a mixture of yesterday's ass and hot garbage.
Usually has severe dandruff and visible ear wax.

How to Deal:
There are several options here. Mouth breathing can help, until you imagine all the funk particles going down your throat without the benefit of nose hair filtration. You could also try cologne dousing, soap beating (maybe he'll get the idea), or blasting his brains out with the fire hose.

The Pathological Liar

Description:
They come in all forms. Here are some samples: short little liars, big fat liars, lyin' ass bitches, lying sacks of shit, and lying fucking assholes.

AKA:
Fibber, Deceiver, Falsifier, Liar Liar Pants on Fire, and Just Plain Old Full-A-Shit.

Reactions:
People originally react to the Liar in astonishment, unaware that they are not telling the truth. Eventually, they find out and take every word with a grain of salt.

How to Deal:
Demand proof. The Liar is used to people rolling with whatever they say so call their bluff. Act totally unimpressed by everything you hear. Always respond with an uninterested, "Oh yeah?" In a short time you will then notice the Liar will stop talking to you all together.

The Whore

Description:
The female Whore wears sexy clothes to work, shows a little too much cleavage and too much leg. The other women talk about what a slut she is and the men talk about what a slut she is and ask if she wants to get a drink after work. The male version is not described here because all men are whores.

Height:
Depends on the heels.

Weight:
Light enough to be sexy.

How to Deal:
This is pretty simple. If you are a single man and not put off by her high turnover, get in there and get some of that! Wear a condom or two. If you are married or in a relationship, take a shower, think about the Whore, and rub that mother out!

The Dork

Description:
Easily identified by his grossly unfashionable clothing, glasses, and tendency to talk incessantly about Lord of the Rings

Passions:
Sci-fi
Periodic table of elements
Studying up on hand muscle control to simulate actual vaginal responses when masturbating

Predators:
Big dumb guys
Ex-athletes
Hot popular women

How to Deal:
It never pays to mistreat the dork because they can be useful at the strangest times. For example, he may have an authentic collection of ninja weapons in his car at all times in case of emergency. Perhaps in his spare time he invents a laser that turns women into nymphomaniacs. Better to play it safe than miss out on cool shit like that.

The Spitter

Ahhh!
Pwew!
Heh! Looks like you accidentally drank from my spit cup!

Description:

The Spitter comes in three main forms: the Tobacco Dipper, the Lugey Leaver, and the Wet Talker. The Tobacco Dipper is usually spotted with an old can of soda around to eject his sludge into. His jeans have snuff rings cut out in the right rear pocket. The Lugey Leaver can be identified by his loud hocker production and launching sounds. The Wet Talker may either be a loud mouth with no control over his saliva or it could be someone with a speech impediment who looks like a lawn sprinkler whenever they hit "S" words and "TH" sounds.

Pros:

The Spitter's extra saliva comes in particularly handy when sealing a slew of envelopes. Also, after a face to face encounter, you have to constantly wipe your glasses, leaving them crystal clear for maximum vision.

Cons:

Besides a wet face and sticky shoes, you have to deal with the sheer nastiness of the Tobacco Dipper. You might think you are grabbing your cup of soda and end up with a mouthful of tobacco, spit, and cancer.

How to Deal:

Carrying a piece of plastic sheeting is a good idea if you are going to have multiple encounters with a Wet Talker. The best way to handle the Tobacco Dipper or Lugey Leaver is with pure isolation. Seal them off in a corner of the workplace, designating it as their spit spot. Let their own excess mouth liquid pile up in the corner until they either clean it or drown in it.

The Mooch

Hey dude, ya got five bucks? I forgot my lunch.
I think you also forgot the money you still owe me from the last four times you "forgot your lunch," DUDE!

Description:
The Mooch never seems to have any money or food, but you know he's hiding a wad of cash somewhere. He just doesn't want to spend it. This guy always uses the term "borrow" when he knows damn well he has no intention of ever paying anything back.

Catch Phrases:
"Hey man can I borrow...."
"Hey man, listen...."

Friends:
Usually seen with the Pathological Liar...and that's about it.

How to Deal:
Whenever the Mooch approaches you, beat him to the punch. Ask HIM if he has any money or food. He will become confused and wonder what is happening. Then, remind him he owes you for the other times you bailed him out. He'll run off, borrow a tissue, and cry in the bathroom.

The Homophobe

Description:
We all know it's the gay in himself that he actually hates, but we're not going to get into all that here. He over compensates his masculinity to the extreme by talking sports, growing facial hair, drinking beer and getting tattoos (usually of barbed wire).

Catch Phrases:
"My ass is exit only."
"No, I don't eat hot dogs, you queer!"

Paradox:
Seen with other like-minded homophobes trying to take their male bonding to the next level, not knowing the next level is actually homosexuality.

How to deal:
Messing with the homophobe is almost too easy. He is so overly sensitized to male contact that all you need to do is touch him. A good ass squeezing should send him into convulsions. If that doesn't work, write him some poetry and give him a wink while he reads it. Just remember to wear a bullet proof vest the next day.

The Muscle Head

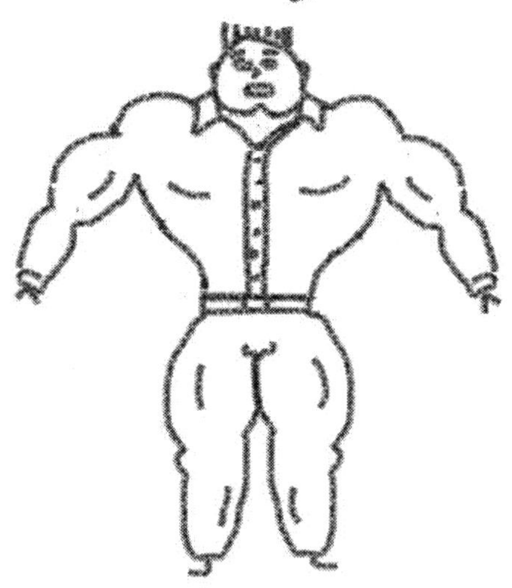

Description:
The Muscle Head is an easy to spot character. He has no neck and arms bigger than most people's legs. He can often be seen mixing a shake with protein powder. He is so strong he is actually less functional because his arms are permanently stuck out a foot and a half from his body.

Warning:
Give the Muscle Head a WIDE berth when he goes to the bathroom. The shakes he drinks might give him enough protein to shit a steak but the smell is so thick and dense, it lowers visibility. Even the Smelly Guy can be heard saying, "Dude! What died in YOUR ass?"

Demeanor:
Ironically, the Muscle Head is usually one of the nicest, most soft spoken guys at work, sometimes with a high voice to boot. But this is due to his complete confidence to effectively pulverize anyone who pisses him off.

How to Deal:
Be friends and kiss ass as much as possible. Tell him your scrawny butt is thinking of working out and ask him for tips. He will be happy to oblige and you can chuckle to yourself as you watch him try to grip a small pen to write down a routine.

Chapter 17

Small Talk and Clichés

"People regurgitate the same old clichés and it becomes like a photocopy of a photocopy of something that's vaguely interesting."

-Steve Coogan

Vaguely interesting is a bit of an overstatement.

Lazy Language

Small talk is lazy language. That's what the workplace does to your brain. Unless you get charged and inspired by your job, your mind is just trying to get through it all. The clichés are sitting in the reserve tank of the brain in order to say SOMETHING, anything at all to avoid just totally ignoring the person and responding with total silence. In a way, it's nothing more than a courtesy reflex. Your creative fun side lays dormant until properly stimulated into action by doing something you actually enjoy.

So let's take a closer look at some of the more frequent cliché expressions that are said in and around the workplace.

"Doing good for a Monday."

Some people let you know they are doing good for a Monday. If it were any other day, they'd be totally lousy, maybe even suicidal, but its Monday and those aren't bad thoughts for such a day.

"Same shit, different day."

What is often neglected in this statement is that often it is the same day but you get different shit, the key word being shit.

"Another day, another dollar."

This phrase is the PG version of same shit, different day. Also, this phrase is literal in many third world countries.

"Have a good day."

People wish this to each other all the time, not because they mean it, but just for the rhythm of the words. "Okay...sounds good. Have a good day! Bye." Hey, we're both at work here, let's not wish each other something that is impossible to attain during this eight hours of the day!

“It is what it is.”

Another thoughtless phrase....it is what it is. Oh yeah? Well, what if you’re wrong and it’s something else? We have a phrase for that too. “Man, that’s something else!” Yeah, it is what it is.

“Tearing a new one.”

“The boss just took him in his office and tore him a new one!” This “one” is a head scratcher. How do you tear someone a new one? You can’t do that! The only thing you can do is tear the one that’s already there. It’s the word “tear” that I have a problem with, it just seems inappropriate. To me, poking a new one would make more sense. Then again, why would you poke a new one? Poke the old one, it’s already there, you know, less work. I sense too much thought went into this.

"Money can't buy you happiness."

Okay, admittedly, this is technically true on the surface. You can't walk into a store and buy a bag of happy. But you know what money can buy you? A whole shitload of other stuff! Money can pay for your shrink and antidepressants, your daily necessities, and fun stuff like bubble gum and bouncy balls. Money can also prevent you from having to do things you hate like going to work every day. So money can't actually buy happiness, but it sure as shit helps.

"Better late than never."

This is true for some things, like menstrual cycles, but not everything. I'm pretty sure it's better when the boss never comes, or the quality inspector, the eviction notice, the police, the apocalypse...

"Think outside the box."

If I was good at thinking outside of the box, do you think I would be in this box to begin with? Now leave me alone, I'm fantasizing about getting into a different kind of box. If the box is a coffin, then we are all thinking outside of the box right now.

"There's no 'I' in team."

Great, you can spell. But I didn't take this job to play on a team. I was done with teams after little league. I took this job because I need money. You know what there is an I in? "I want my paycheck" and "I want you to shut up."

"All work and no play makes Jack a dull boy."

This may be one of the biggest understatements of all time. "All work and no play makes Jack a homicidal pill junkie" might be a bit more accurate. And why doesn't anyone ever talk about the other Jack, the Jack that is all play and no work? He's the awesome Jack that's really fun to be around. That's the Jack we need to care about and aspire to be like.

"Making ends meet."

When I was a kid I thought the phrase was, "Making ends MEAT." To me the phrase meant, I'm only making enough money to buy ass meat. Hey, made sense! I figured ends meat was not the highest quality of meat so a poor person would have to settle for that option. If they couldn't afford ass meat, then they weren't even making ends meat.

"Living the dream."

What dream is that exactly? The one where you're killing zombies with a golf club while your ex-boyfriend yells at you and you can't find your pants?

"Early bird gets the worm."

This phrase tries to reinforce getting up early and starting the day. You are the bird in this analogy. You got up before all the other birds now you have your choice of worms. So if you woke up early and went to the bakery, you weren't complaining that there weren't any damn cinnamon rolls left, like the guy who woke up late. Now what if you were the worm in this scenario? Just out for a morning squirm and some asshole early bird tries to eat you.

"On the ball."

Someone at work might tell you you're really on the ball today. What ball is that exactly? A fitness ball? Do my ab muscles look tight? The eight ball? Are you aware that I'm high on coke? If the job is sedentary, it might be more accurate to say "on your balls." "Wow Ken, I'm impressed with the work you've gotten done at your computer. You've really been on your balls today!"

Chapter 18

Company Jargon

"Incomprehensible jargon is the hallmark of a profession."

- Kingman Brewster, Jr.

What he said.

Mission Statements

Mission statements are about as meaningful as sending a birthday card to a dead person. Anyone can write one and they're about as interchangeable as car commercials. Just throw words like best, excellent, value, and quality into a blender along with the company name and voila! You have your mission statement.

Mission statements are supposed to serve as a reminder of what the company stands for and what its purpose is. It's a nice thought, and it looks good in brochures and other forms of PR, but often it's just not accurate. Businesses regularly fall short of the high standards their mission statements project.

Here is an example of a more honest mission statement: "Our mission is to provide an acceptable product because we manufacture overseas where QUALITY control is a bitch. We also would like to give EXCELLENT customer service, but our people are overworked and underpaid, and thus very prone to bad moods. Finally, we could offer better prices and VALUE but we wouldn't make as much money."

Employees could care less about mission statements. It's the furthest thing from the minds of the workers as they have their own jobs to deal with. If they had their own mission statement it would sound like this: "Despite my misery I will try to get my ass to work and do an EXCELLENT job of pretending to do my duties with just enough QUALITY not to get fired because I VALUE having a paycheck."

Lingo

Every job has industry-specific lingo. Knowing these words makes you an insider, part of a club of which you never wanted to be a member. You could live a full and happy life never knowing any of this jargon, and as a matter of fact, just the sound of these words can induce nausea.

Often this lingo is completely unnecessary, as words already exist in the English language that would suffice. But somewhere along the lines, people that wanted their work to seem more important invented some stupid words for everyone to use. "Hey Mr. Jones, where should I put these boxes?"

"Don't you mean those reusable corrugated storage units?"

"I mean these fucking heavy cardboard boxes that I'm tired of holding, you prick!"

Quality Control

This is an area of the company that deals with maintaining an acceptable level of quality. They check the products to make sure everything is up to standard. The name seems odd to me. It seems like you would have a group of people trying to control all the quality going on so it doesn't spread. You know, like disease, pest, or population control...quality control.

How about a Quality of Life Control for the employees? Maybe a group of people that monitor peoples' lives. "Hey look, 10% of our workforce is on welfare. Maybe we should give them a raise."

Initials & Acronyms

Work is about getting things done fast and as efficiently as possible so we have to be able to convey info quickly. That's where all the abbreviations come into play. "Hey Jameson, did you save the FAQ's for the IRA pamphlet on CD? No? WTF? There wasn't much to do! It wasn't TMI or anything. Get it done ASAP and don't BS me!"

"Boss, I hope you die of HIV, you SOB!"

A as In...

If you have to talk on the phone at all at work, you have to spell things out like a first grader just to convey your message. Everybody seems to use the same alphabetic objects too. That's amazing considering I don't remember having a meeting or anything with the entire human population. A as in Apple, D as in dog, P as in Paul, F as in Frank, and S as in Sam. Those are pretty much the standards. Sometimes you'll get a person who throws a curve ball. "That's P as in psycho." It takes you an extra second to think on that one for some reason. Or you just talk to someone who doesn't know how to spell. "That is Q as in cake." Mmm, okay. Usually these people have an accent and a lot of phlegm in their voice.

Chapter 19

Customer Service

"People forget how fast you did a job - but they remember how well you did it."

- Howard Newton

Unless it was a hand job. Then they remember both.

Service Industry Job

It's practically a rite of passage to work in face-to-face customer service at some point. The following is the definition of a service industry job according to me: a low paying, customer service oriented position in which you take crap from customers and management alike.

Cashier Jobs

A cashier job is something most people have done at some point as well. It's an easy job, if everything goes right. You just have to keep the line moving. Unfortunately, you have to deal with the customers. A lot of people don't show the cashier any respect, even if you are nice to them. "Hello, how are you doing today?"

"I'm in a hurry!"

"Well too bad you picked me, honey, because I'm not! I've got another 4 hours to kill here." Beep!

Fast Food Jobs

If you haven't worked fast food, consider yourself lucky. Low pay, greasy air, uncomfortable uniforms, and on top of everything else, dealing with customers, is part of every day. I think fast food joints are the culmination of lousy in schmoe jobs. I admire anybody who can stick it out and treat customers with respect.

I like the billboards for fast food joints, especially when they show the diversity of the workforce. We see the Asian, the white woman, the black male and female, perhaps an Indian manger in a different shirt and hat, and a white male senior citizen to top things off. What are these billboards for? "Hey! Look at how many different people, from all age groups and walks of life, are working at this horrible place! Why not you? Look how many people are at the end of their rope and this is the last place they can find employment!"

The Customer is Always Right

You've probably heard this phrase already, especially if you've worked in customer service. This phrase had to have been invented by an asshole customer. Those that have served customers know that much of the time the customer is an idiotic douche bag who is quite simply, wrong. They can be rude, impatient, ignorant, misinformed, obnoxious, even dirty and smelly. It's hard to imagine such attributes ever being considered right.

Providing Customer Service to Americans

Our culture is the hardest group of people on the planet to provide customer service to. Why? Because we live in an instantaneous, get whatever you want right now, type of society. People's expectations are out of whack and too high. Anything outside of getting exactly what they want, they get irritated and usually take it out on the wrong person-YOU. Did you make the policy that pisses them off? No, but you are the face of the company. Just out of their convenience you will get yelled at for things beyond your control. Nice, huh?

There are two types of people to serve, high and low maintenance. I suppose there's also mid-maintenance people, but we'll leave them out for the purposes of our discussion. My advice to the high maintenance people is take notes from the low maintenance people. They're not surprised by problems, hassles, and horrible customer service. Low expectations keep them from being disappointed. They're always happy when anything besides a disaster happens. Look into it assholes.

Chapter 20
Inappropriate Behavior

"Nothing is work unless you'd rather be doing something else."

- George Halas

That about sums up most jobs, George

Being Offended

People are so sensitive these days that it's hard to know what will offend them. Since getting offended is totally subjective, just about anything can be considered offensive given the right person or circumstance. You might say something as benign as, “I'm so hungry, I could eat a horse.” But it might be your misfortune that an overly sensitive equestrian was standing nearby, and now she's going to report an equine death threat.

I don’t understand being offended. I’m almost incapable of being offended. Seriously, there is nothing you can say that could offend me. Call me stupid, tell me I’m ugly, my penis is too big etc. I’m fine with it all. Just don’t tell me this book sucks.

Everyone reserves the right not to like something. But if someone says something or treats you in a way you don't appreciate, have the balls and decency to tell them to their FACE. We're all big boys and girls, we can communicate with each other. Don't skip right to reporting them to a superior. Tattle-telling is best left to grade school kids. This is the real world where people need their jobs. Trying to get someone fired for an "inappropriate" comment that hurt your virgin ears is inappropriate in itself, you self-righteous ass.

Sexual Harassment

Sexual harassment is a form of compliment. If you don't like it, stop looking so damn good. Stop wearing the sexy clothing, quit going to the gym and cease bathing.

Personally, I get upset when I am not sexually harassed. Unfortunately no one takes these complaints seriously. I want off-color remarks directed at me and my crotch repeatedly squeezed. If I make it through an entire work day without a single sexual advance, I'm left feeling unwanted and unattractive. I don't care if the attention is from old ladies or even gay dudes. I feel better knowing that at least someone wants to fuck me.

One of the most important factors that affects whether or not a comment or advance is considered sexual harassment is who it comes from. If the six-foot-two, tan, muscular guy slaps a chick on the ass, he's going to get a smile and giggle in return. If I do it, I'm likely to get a slap right back in the face and a meeting with HR.

Sex at Work

Having sex at work is an excellent way to pass the time. It's even better if you do it with a partner. If you're doing it with a coworker, it's pretty much guaranteed to end badly. Not that you shouldn't do it, just be prepared for things to get weird when you are no longer engaging in coitus. This is of course unless you were banging the office whore, then it's business as usual.

Choosing location is key here. The bathroom is an option, but I personally don't find the scent of feces and stale urine an aphrodisiac. In a large conversion van on your lunch break would be nice and comfy, but chances are that if you own one, no one wants to fuck you. On the boss's desk is a classic, especially if it's not even the boss you're having sex with. There is a certain amount of satisfaction that, unbeknownst to your boss, you left a few drops of your genetic code on her workspace.

Gossip

Gossip is simply unavoidable in the workplace. It exists because the fact that Amber is pregnant with someone else's baby and Bruce just came out of the closet is far more for interesting than whatever work you're doing. For some, gossip is what gets them through the day.

The main problem with gossip is its accuracy. If you've ever played the game telephone, you know that the further information travels the more it gets distorted. This is especially problematic when the grapevine is also your source of work-related information because incompetent managers don't tell anyone anything. For example, a new policy may get instituted requiring workers to punch in five minutes before their shift begins. However, because you heard the information second hand, you get fired for punching five women before shitting on their chins.

Swearing

Swearing is one of the most effective ways for schmoes to express themselves. Swear words were likely created by the schmoe out of pain and frustration. Rich people don’t have nearly as much need for swearing. For example, “Ahhh, fuck! I have too much money!” or “Son of a bitch! I don’t need to work for the rest of my life!” Doesn’t sound right, does it? The only way a rich person can sound half normal using swear words is if they were once a schmoe themselves. Schmoes own swear words. They have an intimate relationship with them. Every day, when the schmoe’s alarm clock goes off, the first thing that comes to their mind is “Fuck!” The first thing they say when they pull into work, “Shit!” The first thing they say when they get their paycheck, “Son of a bitch!”

Farting

Working in close proximity to attractive people or customers will often cause the desire to hide your flatulence. This can be tricky if you work in confined areas and/or are a gassy person. How many times have you thought the coast was clear and let one rip only to have someone turn the corner and enter your stink zone?

If you don't care who knows, or if you specifically wish to take credit for the olfactory offense, that is another matter entirely. That's when your ass becomes the fun trumpet. How loud and stinky can it get? Extra points if a mouthful of your colon makes someone puke.

Horseplay

Superiors rarely understand horseplay. They generally try to break it up before it "gets out of hand." What they don't realize is that horseplay functions as a pressure release valve. If you don't let the schmoe blow off a little steam every once in a while, they will eventually explode.

Examples of horseplay:

Wrestling – Wrestling comes in several forms. Some schmoes wrestled competitively when they were younger and enjoy bringing their skills to the workplace. Many schmoes enjoy watching pro-wrestling and have a desire to pile drive or hit someone with a chair. There is also old-fashioned arm wrestling. Whichever form is chosen, they all serve as a reminder that the schmoe is not as young as he used to be and is really out of shape. No match lasts longer than a minute and they all end with both parties lying on the floor gasping for oxygen.

Fart torture – One person farts on another, which results in a chase, usually ending in one of the wrestling forms.

Garbage can basketball – One person's attempt to throw away a crumpled up piece of trash turns into a departmental pickup game. These can get violent, and again, degenerate into wrestling.

Nut-punching - Unguarded jewels can become the victims of a quick backhand by a passing schmoe. A smack-back or, yet again, wrestling ensues.

Fighting

Fights at work nowadays bare little resemblance to "the old days." Years ago, fights were fights. Two guys had a problem, and they settled it with good old fashioned fisticuffs. One guy won, the other lost, conflict resolved, and back to work. Nature took its course. Now these situations are blown way out of proportion. Blows don't even have to be thrown, it could just be two dudes huffing and puffing at each other, and the fallout is almost endless. Be ready for paperwork, reprimands, suspensions, policy changes, departmental meetings, police involvement, legal fees, and anger management. And this is supposed to be seen as progress?

Why does civilization have to equate to more paperwork and less freedom? Why not have some fun with employee conflicts? Every workplace should have a conflict resolution cage for the dudes as well as a mudpit for the ladies. Throw 'em in there and let them battle it out while everyone else takes a break to enjoy the entertainment and have a few beers. Any lost productivity can be offset by alcohol sales and video rights.

The Internet

The internet gives you practically limitless potential to stay distracted at work. From shopping and checking email, to sports and pornography, there is plenty to keep you busy all day long. However, you must be careful to cover your tracks. I was once fired from a job in part for looking at porn on the internet. At the time, I was unaware of how to clear the history on the computer. Nowadays, even clearing the history may not be enough. Information about where you have been online can be stored on the company servers. This is why I recommend going to questionable websites on the computer of a coworker that you don't like. It's harder to trace it back to you, and you might get lucky and get the asshole fired.

Copying Supervisor on Email

If you work in an office, emails are a big part of the job. They are the main route for information passed around and through the office. Sometimes you make a mistake or have to ask a question to another employee. Then they respond and copy your boss on it. That's just one of those little "screw yous" that come up now and again. You didn't HAVE to let the boss in on this but you did anyway. That will sometimes start a cyber carbon copy war between employees. If a war breaks out like that, I suggest a sneak attack in the form of a blind carbon copy.

What I like when two people are fighting through email at work is that the language they use is professional but firm and it makes for good reading, if you are on the outside of the situation.

"Kate: The policy is quite clear in saying that we can NOT issue an off cycle check to an employee on an unpaid administrative leave, even for time already worked before the leave began. If you are having trouble understanding or need someone to clarify the policy for you please let me know. I will be happy to go over it with you, AGAIN."

Ouch!

Suppressed Laughter

There is something about the simple fact of not being allowed to laugh that makes you want to laugh that much harder. The quieter and more serious the environment is, the more the mind wants to play. You picture something funny or something is said that makes you want to laugh your ass off. It gets even better when the person next to you is having the same problem. You can't even look at each other without cracking up.

You have to find ways to stifle those laughs in the midst of a serious discussion. No one wants to be the person that busts up in the middle of a lecture on rape (as I and another person came within a hair of doing during jury duty, one of the most beautiful memories I have regarding suppressed laughter). Some people will try to fake a sneeze or release the laugh through their nose but that runs the risk of producing a high velocity snot rocket. Depending on where that sucker lands, you may be wishing you had just laughed. Another way of getting the laugh out is to pretend you are crying. This only works if the subject matter fits into your reaction. If you are talking about numbers or going over policies, crying won't work no matter how hard you try to make it fit. "My mother showed me a presentation with graphs like that on her death bed."

Chapter 21
Time Off

"A vacation is what you take when you can no longer take what you've been taking."

- Earl Wilson

If you're a schmoe, you've been taking a lot, right in the ass.

Smoke Breaks

Some consider smoking unhealthy, and it certainly can be. But a shitty job is also very unhealthy. So when you take a break from work to smoke a cigarette, they sort of cancel each other out. Yes, you are sucking carcinogens into your lungs, but if that short break from work helps to keep you from killing yourself or someone else, well then it can't be that unhealthy can it?

Smoke breaks can feel a little unfair to the non-smoker. That's why the non-smokers need to take "talk to the smokers" breaks. Grab a pack of candy cigs and pretend you're a smoker. While they get their nic fix, you can get a sugar rush. You should actually take more breaks than the smokers to make it fair because they're going to have a lot of time off when they get lung cancer.

Unfortunately for the smoker, it has become increasingly difficult to have smoke breaks. If it hasn't gotten harder to find the time, it has definitely gotten harder to find the place. Back in the olden days, you could smoke right at your desk. Shit, doctors could smoke in their offices. Soon, however, it became regulated to specific areas, like the break room. These designated areas have become more and more remote, so that now, you have to leave the building entirely and even stay a certain distance from it. Before long, smokers will have to drive to an Indian reservation to smoke. Oh well, longer smoke breaks. "Hey, your paycheck says you worked last week. I don't remember seeing you here."

"I was on a smoke break."

Vacation

What you get out of your vacation depends on how you feel about your life. If you are content with where you are, then a vacation is just a little sprinkle of spice on top of your life. If you are a working schmoe whose soul is being sucked out everyday, a vacation is an absolute necessity. It's usually one week to get yourself back together, to go nuts and to live the way you want to. The problem is coming home. For the person happy with your life, there is little difference in coming back to work. They make the transition seamlessly. The schmoe, on the other hand, rather than feel refreshed, feels like they need another vacation!

Really the only thing the schmoe can do is vacation in horrible places around the globe. That way when they come home it will seem like an improvement. People will notice the difference in you around the workplace. "Hey Tom, you really look rested. Where was it you went again...Myrtle Beach?"

"Ah, no actually, we went to Darfur, in Sudan. Yeah, we took the genocide package. It was a good time. We stayed at a refugee camp in Chad. The kids had a good time. They learned to shoot AK-47's, how to yodel in Arabic, and use camel dung as fuel. I had to sell Jennifer into slavery so we could bribe our way back across the border but I'm working with the Swiss Embassy to get her back."

Holidays

Oftentimes the schmoe is forced to work on a holiday when they would rather be with family and friends. Yes, you may make time and a half or double time, but this still doesn't compensate for the triple or quadruple pain that you feel for having to be there.

The schmoe, of course, loves any holiday that gets them off work with pay. They don't have to agree with it, they don't have to believe in it, they don't even have to know what or who it's about. As long as they don't have to go to work, the schmoe will happily celebrate that holiday. They might celebrate Hitler's birthday if it meant a day off with pay.

Working Sick

For most of us, long gone are the days of staying home as long as we needed, with mom bringing us hot soup as we watched cartoons. Instead, it's a slug of medicine for breakfast and off to operate heavy machinery to bring home that paycheck.

If a strict boss is the main reason for you having to work sick, take the time to make sure they are well aware of your illness. A nice sneeze to the face or barf to the chest should get the point across.

As a schmoe, you understand that people often must suck it up and come to work sick. Somehow that doesn't seem to make it more bearable when you're stuck working next to a diseased coworker. "Gee, thanks for coming in to share your bubonic plague with me. I've been feeling too healthy lately and needed a good illness to burn up my sick days. Dick."

The Art and Science of Calling Off

There are times (like every morning) that you don't feel like heading into work. You might be prompted to call off. Some people can do that with ease, conscience free. The rest of us, with a modicum of a work ethic, have trouble making that call if it's really nothing greater than, "I just don't feel like going in."

There is always the sick voice. This is something that you rehearse before you make that call. Incidentally, we find it best to make that call as soon as you wake up. The sick voice will be aided by the morning rasp and phlegm that accumulated naturally overnight. Just be warned that you will probably have to act a little sick the next day at work.

Basically it all comes down to lying. That's all calling off is when you don't really need to. The question you need to ask yourself is, what form should the lie take? If you aren't going to use sickness for yourself, this is where having kids helps. Just tell the boss your kid is sick and bam, you are home for the day. We should mention that the smaller the child, the more believable this lie is. You don't want to call your boss, tell him your kid is sick, and then have him remember that you invited her to your son's college graduation five years earlier.

Don't get too complicated either. A call off should be under

90 seconds. A lot of times we feel that if we bombard the boss with details, then the lie is more believable. Not always true. If we were better liars we might be independently wealthy, so stick to the basics.

Getting Off Work When You're Out of Time Off

If you have used all your time off, but you still need some time away, here's what you do. Don't show up, don't call in, in fact have a family member call your boss and ask if they have seen you there. After you take your desired time off, come back to work in the clothes you last wore there but have them covered in mud and torn up. Have broken ropes around your wrists and ankles. Then just walk to your boss's office crying and apologizing. Be incoherent with your story if you're asked what happened. Mention a windowless van, a mustache, and sob uncontrollably. That should be enough to satisfy your boss's curiosity. Not only will you not be questioned about the time you missed, you will get sent you home for a few more days. That'll give you enough time to conjure up the full lie.

10 Excuses for Calling Off

1. I read The Little Engine That Could and it left me feeling like I couldn't.
2. I have a doctor's excuse for a bad itch that would be inappropriate to scratch at work.
3. 21 words. I was babysitting my friend's monkey. If there is one animal you don't want to leave unattended, it's monkeys, my friend.
4. I didn't realize how sticky super glue really is. At least I was stuck by the phone so I could call off and you'd know what happened.
5. I'm going through a leisure phase at the moment.
6. A bird pooped on my door handle. I'll be in when/if It rains.
7. My work-induced dementia is kicking in. I don't remember if I even have a job.
8. I have to break in my new couch.
9. I'm looking for meaning in my life right now, my job is meaningless, so I'm staying away from there!
10. I'm a little emotional because my bed is so warm and cozy, it feels like a womb, and it's making me miss my mother's uter-us.

Chapter 22

Amenities and Perks

"Luck is the dividend of sweat. The more you sweat, the luckier you get."

-Ray Kroc

That is so true. One time I was in a sauna and got lucky.

The Break Room

A break room should have:

- Comfortable couches
- Big screen TV
- Cable
- Internet
- Clean appliances
- Well stocked refrigerator, including fine imported beers
- Nudie magazines
- Arcade games

A break room usually has instead:

- A shitty table
- Plastic lawn chairs
- A dirty microwave with several years of food spatter
- A filthy refrigerator with condiments left over from an earlier generation of workers
- A black and white TV from the pre-remote control era

Cafeterias

Some employers do not permit their employees to leave for

lunch. This is not only cruel and unusual, but probably illegal. It forces you to either pack your lunch or eat at the company cafeteria. This is akin to the company store of the days of old that charged high prices to get their wages back and keep people essentially as indentured servants.

Eating in a work cafeteria is like high school all over again. The cliques, the gossip, the people who no one wants to sit with, and the shitty food are all there. If it's going to be like high school, might as well act like it. Throw food, shoot spitballs, and make your friends laugh until chocolate milk comes out their noses. Live it up like the only consequence is detention, and don't forget to go back to "class" late.

The Proverbial Water Cooler

The water cooler has long been known as a special gathering place in the workplace. Jokes are told, rumors exchanged, even arguments are waged, all over small paper cups of water. It is a rendezvous of thirsty minds, the importance of which should not be understated. The dildo may have been invented in front of a water cooler.

There's an easy way to make the water cooler a more interesting place. Just get a couple bottles of grain alcohol or vodka and spike that sucker. Use it as a tool to loosen up even the tightest of assholes. When the prudes want to know why the water tastes bad, tell them its a special vitamin and mineral blend for optimum health and productivity. Before you know it, they'll be hanging up disco balls and strobe lights and photocopying their bare asses.

The Vending Machine

A sample transaction: You arrive at the vending machine only to find that the item you wanted is sold out. Motherfucker! Now you must make an alternate and less satisfying selection. You choose, and then you notice that the exact change only light is on. You don't have exact change, you only have dollar bills. At this point, you decide you are hungry enough to sacrifice the paltry change that would come your way. You put the dollar in the slot, and... it comes back out at you. You turn it around the other way and try again. Rejected again. After two or three more tries, you start systematically trying all the dollars in your wallet. None are accepted. You begin to iron the current dollar against the side of the machine. Still no luck. Out of frustration, you swear and ball up the dollar in your sweaty, angry fist. Before you walk away, you try the moist, crumbled dollar one last time. You're in! Time to push the button. Fuck! You pushed the wrong button! Now, instead of the candy bar you wanted you are getting a bag of cheese puffs. But wait, the puffs get stuck. Now you are faced with yet another quandary. Spend more money and get two, cut your losses and let some other lucky asshole get one for free, or shake the living shit out of the machine to try to get it to drop. You're too weak from hunger to act like you're wrestling a bear so you decide on buying two. Two of the crap that you didn't want in the first place. The bags drop, and you grab one and rip it open. One bite and you discover they're stale as shit. In the trash it goes and you're on your way back to work ... hungry.

Employee Discounts

Employee discounts can be a nice little perk sometimes. I say little, because often the discount is quite limited. They have to profit from the employees, right? Still, even a small discount adds up, especially if you work somewhere that you can buy necessities. But you're out of luck if say, you have all your limbs, and you work at a prosthetic factory. I guess it could be useful for gifting if you know some amputees.

Some people will take jobs specifically for the employee discount to help support whatever addiction they may have. Shoes, underwear, cheeseburgers - whatever they crave, practically their entire paycheck goes back to the company. This is precisely why I could never work in a bakery, brewery, or brothel.

Employee of the Month

If you want to honor someone for a job well done, putting their picture up for coworkers to draw on and make fun of probably isn't the way. The premium parking is nice, but let's get rid of the public humiliation.

When you do the math, employee of the month isn't really fair. Suppose you win employee of the month in February, and it's not even leap year? Your reign as company dork is cut short by a couple of days. Meanwhile some other assbag wins during a 31-day month and gets three more days of sweet parking than you. Maybe they should pick a dependable female employee on birth control and go by her menstrual cycle instead.

Birthdays

What do you get from work on your birthday? A shitty cake? Maybe if you're lucky or have nice coworkers. Most employers don't know when your birthday is and don't care. It's not that I think birthdays need an elaborate celebration - I don't like getting older so I generally don't like being reminded of my birthday. But I figure if you're still alive and showing up for work, some kind of birthday perk would be nice. Maybe a bottle of wine, hooker, or best of all, a paid day off. At the very least, how about a full day of not giving you any shit? Birthdays serve as another reminder of the years of your life that you're giving to the company. Certainly that deserves more than a store-bought confection.

Seniority

In schmoe jobs, people love pulling rank. Whether it comes to picking vacation days, choosing shifts or even choosing jobs, the preference generally goes by seniority. If you're on the beneficial end of this, it provides a tiny counterbalance to all those shitty working years. If you're one of the newer workers, however, be prepared to get the shaft. The big, cranky old shaft from the workers that have been there longer and have already clawed their way through the abuse of their seniors. And if you work at a place where employees rarely leave, get nice and comfy with that shaft because you pretty much have to wait for someone to die off before you can move up in the ranks.

Casual Fridays

Woohoo! It's party time, baby! Talk about cutting loose! I'm wearing jeans in the workplace. Nothing can hold me back now! I practically feel like I'm not even working thanks to the magic of denim!

Casual Friday doesn't necessarily have to refer to your clothing. Try coming to work with a casual attitude. "Aaron, you've been very careless and apathetic today. What's the problem?"

"It's casual Friday and I'm behaving accordingly. Now fuck off."

Employees Only!

In the workplace there are often doors that have the mighty words "Employees Only" on them. As a kid you might have wondered what kind of cool stuff could be in there. Ninjas? Candy? Naked girls? Naked ninja girls eating candy? But to your dismay, only employees were deemed worthy to walk through that space in the wall. As a grown up schmoe, you become all too familiar with the misery, low pay, and abuse you must endure to enter employee only areas. It turns out it's not very cool at all in there. No magic or fairy dust, mostly just fat guys, boxes, and butt cracks.

Chapter 23
Restrooms

"Laziness may appear attractive, but work gives satisfaction."

- Ann Frank

So does a good bowel movement.

The Restroom

So let me get this straight, just because I work with these people, I have to shit next to them too? What is this, prison? It can make for many awkward moments when you step out and see one of your co-workers. You look each other in the eye and both know that you stunk up the whole fucking place. It's especially embarrassing when you are in the wrong restroom. Well, you can't flush your tampon down the urinal, can you?

White Noise and Restrooms

I worked in an office that pumped in white noise into our work area. It was kind of a static, air whooshing type of sound. I asked why we do that and the boss told me it's to muffle people's voices. You know where we didn't have it? In the bathroom! Listen, I don't mind hearing people talk but I DO mind hearing their business hit the water!

Restrooms are the quietest places on Earth and I never understood why. They are quieter than a library. Maybe that's why people read in there, I don't know. You tell me we can't extend the music wire from the lobby into the bathroom to soften the blow a little? Fucking elevators have music! But no, not the restroom. In there I have to listen to a stranger's pee tap dance across the bowl water. I don't want that! I don't want to hear someone's asshole pooch open. Every stall should be like a soundproof room. Either that or throw some heavy metal on. That way you can shit, fart, piss, & puke as loud as you want to.

Toilet Paper

Why must companies pad their bottom lines by irritating ours? The sorry excuse for TP they buy to save money is often one step away from sandpaper. We're not woodworking in there, so how about something a little more cushiony than 80-grit for our bums?

I bring baby wipes with me, nothing but the best for my corn hole. Some people find this strange. But as my esteemed brother has pointed out, if you got poo on your arm, for example, hopefully you wouldn't think a couple wipes with dry paper would suffice. Why should the anus be treated with less respect?

Substandard Facilities

Dropping a deuce at work can be a relaxing way to waste some time, that is unless the bathroom at your workplace is so nasty that the cockroaches won't use it. I've definitely worked some jobs where finding a tree or wearing diapers were more appealing options than the bad plumbing or the port-a-pottie overfilled with Mt. Poopmore.

The reason why bathrooms stay nasty, besides the obvious fact they don't get cleaned enough, is they get caught in a vicious cycle. The worse the bathroom is, the less people feel the need to clean up after themselves. "There's pee on the seat and floor? Eh, what's a little more gonna hurt? There's writing on the wall? I'd better finish some of these sentences." It can seem like as long as the waste gets into the bathroom, actually hitting the proper receptacles is an afterthought. No one gives a shit where they leave a shit.

Segregation

The chasm between the blue and white collar is reminiscent of the days before the civil rights movement. Obviously during those times it was far worse for blacks, but today the blue collar schmoe is a sort of pseudo-black in the workplace. Separate bathrooms and break rooms, different attire, special rules...the list goes on of the ways we schmoes are put in our place. At one of my jobs, I was kicked out of two different premium bathrooms. My waste was unauthorized and apparently unworthy to be deposited in those locations. On the one hand I can understand and appreciate the desire of the workplace elite to protect their turf. But as a schmoe doing their grunt work, I just want to shit in it.

The Janitor/Cleaning Crew

There are two types of people in the world: those who use the toilets and those who clean them. Actually, I suppose those who clean the toilets need to use them too. Also, those who use them have to clean them at home. I guess there are a lot of people in this world and everybody uses and cleans toilets so please disregard my opening.

Anyway, being someone in the workplace who has been the cleaner of toilets, I can honestly say that people look at you a little differently, if they look at you at all. I felt low cleaning the area where someone dropped bombs, or worse, while they were currently dropping them. The custodians often get the least amount of respect, but deserve the most considering what they have to deal with. So learn the crew by name and treat them with dignity. They'll appreciate that over being ignored or looked down upon. When you are in a stall call out to the dude in there cleaning, "Hey Mike, here's to job security." Grunt. Plop. Flush.

As someone who cleaned both men and women's bathrooms, I can honestly say that the women's was much dirtier. We would clean the bathrooms FOUR times a day. Each time it looked like the shit fit brigade came in for a rave. I was amazed at all the places you could get excrement. They had to be artists or something to get that creative. I just imagined a nude trapeze act swinging around in the stall, just letting everything fly where physics dictated.

Chapter 24

Smells at Work

"A man who works hard stinks only to the ones that have nothing to do but smell."

- Laura Ingalls Wilder

And men don't care how hard a woman works as long as she looks and smells good.

Olfactory Cornucopia

The smells at work, no matter where you are employed, run the full range from pleasant to puke-inducing. You might work with some lovely ladies who leave a nice light scent of perfume or shampoo in their wake. Mmm, now that's a nice experience. A moment later you're in the break room at lunch time and get the waft of frozen, microwave dinner, cheese smell. How ironic, here you are about to eat your lunch and the smell of food is going to make you lose your appetite. No need to even mention restrooms in the workplace again!

Then you have unexpected smells that may or may not brighten your day. Let's say you open a new ream of paper and get a nice whiff of fresh paper smell. Ahhh, that's nice. Or maybe some copier toner is your thing. Perhaps you got some gas that day and got some on your hands, now you can carry it with you and get a little high, makes for a more pleasant and savory day.

Bad Breath

Of course the smelly guy has bad breath. That is expected. However, bad breath can happen even to the best of us from time to time. Dehydration, the occasional tuna sandwich, or even a romp with the whore can be causes of bad breath. Depending on your level of comfort with coworkers, this can be a touchy subject to deal with. If you're close friends, you can always be straightforward. "Dude, your mouth smells like a dumpster filled with dead rodents." Your friend will thank you for the heads up, and he can fix the problem before talking to a sexy coworker.

If you are not close friends, however, it is safer to use more indirect methods. For example, you can always use the old trick of pulling out a mint or stick of gum for yourself and offering some to the owner of the offending mouth. Unfortunately, they often turn it down, not catching the hint. The next step is to try to sell it to them. "This gum is awesome! You've never had it before?" To this, you may get a reply like, "No, I'm not a big gum person." To that, you'd like to say, "Well no shit! Judging by the smell of your mouth, you're not a big oral hygiene person in general." After a few tries on the sell, if they still don't take it, it's time to accept the fact that they're gonna stink and walk away. A nose-friendly conversation is never going to happen.

Cologne and Perfume

We all prefer our coworkers to smell pleasant. But when it comes to artificial body scent enhancement, I'm with the school of thought that less is more. I don't find it enjoyable when someone smells like they were standing too close to a toxic chemical spill. A good rule of thumb is that if the air around you is flammable, you've used too much. I'm not sure why some people douse themselves to such an offensive degree. Maybe they have some of their own stink they're trying to cover up, or maybe they think this will attract the opposite sex. If by attract, they mean "to make pass out," then I guess it works.

The Employee Coat Rack

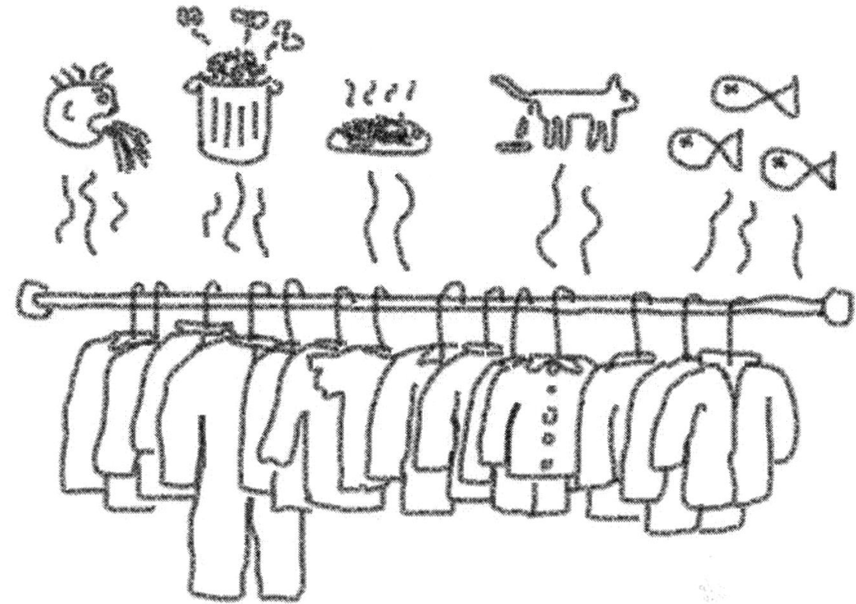

Depending on where you work, and more importantly, who you work with, the coat rack can be one nasty cluster-fuck. As you walk past, you get inundated with a cornucopia of unpleasant smells like wet dog, smoke, bacon, perfume, cat pee, vomit, and semen. The commiseration of your coat with the others can cause you to go home with some unwanted odors. You may have started your shift with chicken soup, but now you're ending it with your wife wanting to know why you smell like Rita's rump roast.

Your coat is also vulnerable to other dangers like employees with sticky fingers. I mean this both literally and figuratively. Along with missing personal effects, you might also find gooey hand prints. My advice is to either leave the coat in the car or wear a coat that no one would want to fuck with. Put items like live crabs in your pockets and sew a big patch on the back that says "Head Lice Rule!" If someone steals your coat after that, you don't want it back.

Chapter 25
Keeping Your Job

"Of all the aspects of social misery nothing is so heartbreaking as unemployment."
- Jane Addams
No, running out of unemployment checks is more heartbreaking.

Job Security

Job security may have existed at one time, but now the only job security I'm aware of is when you get laid off and security escorts you out of the building. Schmoes are as expendable as dirty diapers, and there's always more schmoes lined up behind you to take your job, probably for less money.

The best job security the schmoe can have is the ability to blackmail superiors and coworkers. Having dirt on as many people as possible is the best weapon against job loss. "Hey Boss, you say there is the possibility of lay offs? We wouldn't want everyone to know about your affair with the secretary as well as your raging hemorrhoid problem? I didn't think so. I'll see ya tomorrow."

Pay Cuts

In a world where pay cuts exist, it is no surprise that people occasionally go postal. Nothing says insult quite like getting paid less money to do the same job. Some might argue that at least you still have a job, but I think it may be more humane to cut you loose so you can at least collect unemployment while you search for and hopefully find a better job.

If you receive a cut in pay, be sure to reduce your efforts by at least the same percentage. If you were making $10 and they cut you back to $8, be sure to give them no more than 80 percent of your effort. I must specify that this is 80 percent of your previous effort, not of total possible effort. Under no circumstances should you give your employer 100 percent of yourself. Maximum effort given to an employer should hover around half-assed. In the above example we are reducing that by 20 percent, thus total effort should not exceed 40 percent of an ass.

Downsizing

Downsizing is one of many corporate euphemisms used because it sounds better than "firing a bunch of people." They want people to think of good things like efficiency and organization instead of the number of people thrust into unemployment.

If you ever fall victim to downsizing, you can help the executives to experience some downsizing of their own. Break into their houses and offices, steal their stuff, and ice the cake by chopping their legs off. "How's that for downsizing, bitch!"

Unions

Unions are the schmoe's way of getting back at the man. They say, “The man's been fucking us for years. It's high time we start fucking the man. Let's make him pay us more money for doing less work. Let's make it damn near impossible to get fired.”

Companies were corrupt so people and workers came together and unionized for better working conditions. Now unions are powerful and corrupt and forcing companies elsewhere to set up shop. So instead of better working conditions we're getting NO working conditions. Good job guys, keep up the good work. Hey I have an idea, how about an unemployment union?

Strikes

Sometimes a union will go on strike if their demands are not met or terms aren't to their liking, sounds pretty sweet to me. Don't like the work situation? Then don't go in! There's no pay but hey, there's no work either.

When there's a strike we might imagine people chanting and marching in circles with picket signs. Instead we often see them on the side of the road barbequing with a cooler full of beer. How can you NOT feel sorry for their plight? They don't exactly look like starving children now, do they? You see their nice trucks, well fed bellies, and top of the line outdoor furniture and think, "I don't have sympathy for them at all." That's weird, isn't it?

Cheap Labor & Space

My biggest fear is that the only reason we are exploring space is to find cheaper labor. I imagine some guy in a board room saying, you know, these Chinese are making too much money! We need higher profit margins, so what can we do about it? Somebody call NASA!

They say they are looking for life on other planets. True, they are, to make our stupid shit....cheap! Pretty soon you will see labels on your stuff that says, "Made on Enceladus." And you know damn well that Enceladusian stuff won't last. They'll tell us they do the jobs Earthlings won't do and that it's cheaper to ship it for a year than to make it here.

Relocation

Sometimes if you want to keep your job you're forced to relocate. It may be across town or across the country, gotta love being uprooted away from friends and family in order to continue doing something you didn't like in the first place.

Another type of person that commonly gets relocated is a

prisoner. This is no coincidence, for if you have a job you are a prisoner to it. Your crime? The need to make a living.

There are times when the move turns out to be a good thing. You're like an inmate who gets a transfer to minimum security or a nicer facility. Maybe there's better food, nicer company, and a little less rape. But of course, in the end, you're still in jail.

Subcontracting

This is the employer's ingenious way to get you to do all the labor associated with working for the man without any of the benefits. You do everything an employee does except you are not technically an employee. No sick days, holiday pay, vacation, health insurance, or birthday party. The man saves lots of cash, and for you to make it worthwhile you have to be very creative with your taxes.

The good thing is you can't technically get fired, you can only lose your contract. So you can leave that "job" as colorfully as you'd like with no need to mention any firings on future job applications. You might want to skip them as a reference, though.

Chapter 26

Above and Beyond

"To find joy in work is to discover the fountain of youth."
- Pearl S. Buck
No wonder why no one's ever found the fountain of youth.

Workaholics

This I cannot understand for the life of me. Alcoholics I understand. "Mmmm, beer taste good. Ahhh, beer make me feel good and forget about bad. Me drink beer all the time." Makes sense. But what makes someone want to work all the time? Perhaps they hate their spouse and kids, or maybe all that waits for them at home is loneliness. Whatever their reason, to each their own. Since they're at it, they can do my work too and I'll do the staying home for the both of us. I'll pick up the paychecks too. If they're having so much fun I'm sure they're not interested in money.

Based on how the word workaholic was derived, it actually makes it sound like people are addicted to a substance called "workahol." That would be some nasty shit, wouldn't it? It would taste like crap, make you irritable and tired, the effects would last all day, and it would leave you feeling like you never wanted to do it again. But somehow, there are douche bags that would still manage to get addicted to it.

I Love My Job!

I'll hear someone say the following phrase every once in a while. "I love my job." Wow! Really? How? My mind will not allow the concept of love and job be joined together in matrimony. When someone says that to me, I ask for clarification. "So you're saying that you don't mind going to your place of employment? Not only that but you love going, is that correct?"

"Yes it is."

Then my eye starts twitching uncontrollably. We should probably make fun of this type of person more because they will NEVER buy this book. They would be just as bewildered by the concepts here as I am of their love of employment.

Ways to identify this strange breed of human:

- Frequent smiling
- Experiencing satisfaction from their work
- Staying late for reasons other than needing money
- Bringing treats for their coworkers
- Coming to work 15-30 minutes before their shift
- Packing a healthy, well-balanced, carefully prepared lunch
- Skipping instead of walking
- Participating in meetings with enthusiasm
- Keeping neat work spaces
- Not reading this book

Questions During Meetings

Why? Why is it that you always have one person in a meeting that has to ask a bunch of useless questions? There is a subject being discussed and someone is asking about a completely different topic. "So does anyone have any questions about the email formatting? Yes, Farkis?"

"Are we going to have to pay for parking when we move downtown?"

"You're a douche, Farkis."

This is the same person that continues to ask questions as time ticks away past five o'clock, keeping you all hostage until the barrage is done.

Taking Work Home

No! No! No! This is unacceptable and must be avoided at all costs. Home is meant to be a place you completely forget about work, as if it doesn't even exist. The work-home boundary must be maintained. You cannot allow any part of your job to penetrate that perimeter. Once one little piece of work gets in, it multiplies and keeps coming back like a herpes outbreak.

Mandatory Optional Extra Work

Sometimes bosses have a way of asking you to work overtime that makes it sound like you actually have a choice in the matter. They might say something like, "Yeah, I was wondering if you could stay over today?" When they ask this you know damn well you have no choice unless you want to start looking for another job. So you say something like, "Yes, I can stay," when in your mind you're thinking, "No I can't fucking stay! I've already been here for 8 hours, I hate you, I hate this place, and I had plans. Sure, my plans were to go home and do nothing, but damn it, I was excited about those plans!"

Chapter 27

Getting out of Work

"Work is accomplished by those employees who have not yet reached their level of incompetence."

- Lawrence J. Peter

Indeed, fucking off properly takes experience.

Leaving Work Early

Some days are worse than others and you may feel you want to go home early? What are you going to do to accomplish this? Basically I mean, what kind of lie are you going to use? If you go for illness, opt for diarrhea. Diarrhea always wins out. No one will call you out on it, no one will want to talk about it, and they just want you out of there. Work is a game of Rock, Paper, Scissors. Don't play the game by those options. Choose diarrhea. I'm willing to bet that even the president does that now and again. "Sir, your military advisers are waiting in the Oval Office."

"Tell them I have diarrhea."

Now THAT is an exit strategy.

Avoiding Responsibility

The longer you work for a company, the more responsibility they will try to give you. It is an uphill battle to keep your responsibilities to a minimum. You must perform your tasks just well enough so you don't get fired, but not so well that your good work gets noticed.

It is also best to keep any special skills a secret. If it is found out that you can do other things, you will be called upon to do those things. Mention you like to tinker around with computers, and guess what? You're a poor man's tech support. Tell someone you once did some of your own plumbing? Guess who's fixing the clogged toilet?

Even better than hiding skills, is deliberately botching tasks. If you are given a new task and you complete it poorly, there is a good chance they won't ask you to do it again. This also translates into your domestic capacity as well. This is a well-known trick to keep your spouse from giving you extra crap to do.

Pretending to Work

Let's face it, there are times when there just isn't anything to do. Developing the skill of looking busy is incredibly useful for these times. This helps you avoid a boss's request to pretend you're working, or worse, the assignment of busy work. If these sick-minded individuals catch you idle, the next thing you know you might find yourself cleaning between the slots of box fan screens with a toothbrush. Ultimately, the methods you use to look busy depend on your job and creativity. Just remember not to defeat the purpose by making sure that the effort of looking busy does not exceed the effort of actual work.

Disappearing

Even better than looking busy, is disappearing altogether. You certainly can't get more work to do if no one knows where you are. The ease with which you can do this obviously depends on a number of factors. Small people like Asians and midgets are at an advantage as they can wedge themselves into cabinets and other small nooks. Perhaps you could camouflage yourself so that you look like a bookshelf or blend into a chair. You might get lucky and have a sexy coworker accidentally sit on you. Of course, it could also be a fat guy who hasn't recently bathed.

Sleeping on the Job

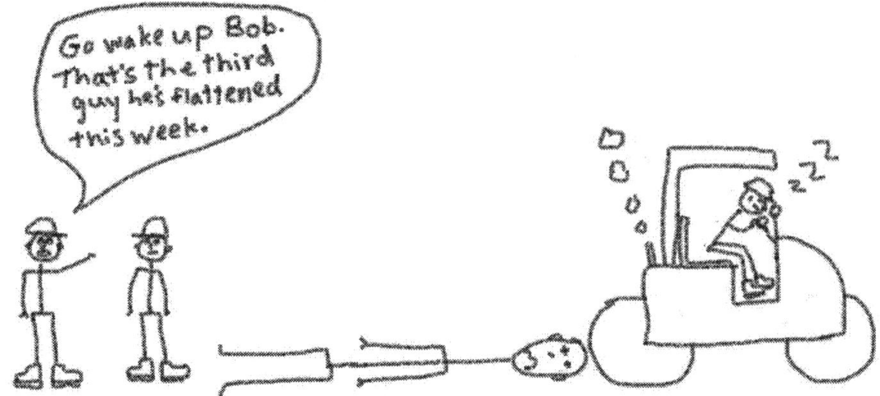

As far as work is concerned, there is hardly a better feeling than sleeping on the job. You're enjoying lala land and getting paid for it all the while. There's an old army adage about not staying awake if you have the opportunity to sleep. I couldn't agree more. Its nice to come home from work feeling rested.

I have long fantasized of a job in which you specifically got paid for sleeping. That would be your only responsibility, coming in and climbing in bed. Better yet, work from home. I wouldn't mind putting in an eight hour day. Shit, I'll do twelves, doubles, weekends, holidays. I'm a company man in this case.

10 Excuses for Leaving Work Early

1. I'm planning on calling off tomorrow and I want to get an early start.
2. I accidentally thought I should leave at 9am.
3. I'm getting a prostate exam and the doctor closes at 4 but my ass closes at 1, so I'm leaving at 10.
4. My dog called. He had the puppies!
5. 8 hours of half-assed work is really just 4 hours, so I'm leaving at noon to save time.
6. I'm going postal, not like that, just need to drop off a package.
7. I got some religious thing going on.
8. I got some gay thing going on.
9. I got some minority thing going on.
10. You're wife is expecting me, since you're at work and have no idea we're fucking. Shhh.

Chapter 28

Leaving a Job

"If at first you don't succeed, try, try again. Then quit. There's no point in being a damn fool about it.

- W.C. Fields

Yep.

Two Week Notice

Have you ever put in your two week notice at the interview? I've done that. You know, you go through the whole process and decide you can't stomach another job right now. They look at you and say, "Well, I think we'd like to extend an offer."

"Actually, I've got some bad news for you. This just isn't working out for me..."

Quitting and Lying

Sometimes you say things out of spite when you put in your two week notice. Maybe you told your boss and coworkers that you are leaving for higher pay and less work at a company that provides paid BJ's on lunch hour. You tell that lie for two weeks and something funny happens...you begin to believe the lie!

On your last day you say your good-byes and drive off, happy to be embarking on your new career. As the celebration dies down in your car, you being to realize that there is no higher paying job. There is no company providing paid BJ's. No, you realize you have to pay for them yourself and, in fact, no longer have any income.

Retirement

Every schmoe hopes to retire early enough to enjoy at least a few years of good health before he dies. This can prove to be difficult. How many times have you heard about the guy that retires only to die of a heart attack or cancer a few months later? At least the company can sleep easy knowing that they got about as much work out of him as they possibly could. Some people just never seem to retire because they can't afford it. You have people in their 70's still humpin' it, and when asked, "When are you going to retire and take it easy?", you may get an answer like, "Ahhh, I'll sleep when I'm dead." They have clearly given up all hope. The rarest situation of all is early retirement. Usually what this means is that they died while still working.

Quitting When You're Younger

You've probably noticed that if you were to look back on your life, that you had more jobs when you were younger. Quitting a job abruptly goes hand and hand with youth. It's part of being a rebel. When you make minimum wage, it can't be any worse anywhere else, just a matter of degree.

When you get older and have more responsibilities, you also start to make a little more money. This can be a trap. You might get to the point of having more vacation and other perks. By then there is much more to risk when quitting a job. It makes you yearn for your younger days.

Permanent Disability Benefits

This is like hitting the injury lottery. Hopefully you're injured just enough to get the benefits, but not so much that you can't do things you enjoy like drink beer and have sex. If you're stuck paralyzed, shitting your pants in a wheelchair while your spouse is off cheating on you, that sucks. Hopefully if that's the case you've gotten a huge settlement so you can hire lots of sexy nurses to give you sponge baths all day.

The Lottery

The biggest insult to the lottery-playing schmoe are the dumb asses who actually do win the lottery, then go broke soon after. These people have the dream in the palm of their hands and they piss it all away. Millions of dollars is a lot of money, yes, but it is not an infinite amount of money. It will run out if you spend it like a jackass. If you're getting by in a small house or apartment before you win, after you win what makes you think you need a 1.2 million dollar mansion, 17 cars, horses, lions, and a roller coaster? If spent wisely, you and your family could live comfortably for the rest of your lives without working another day. When people win the lottery, before they receive their winnings they should have to pass a dumb ass test. If they fail, they should be forced to relinquish the money to a schmoe that can handle it.

I don't like to play the lottery because if you play enough, math dictates that the house always wins. However, I never pass up an invitation into a pool toward a large jackpot. I consider it suicide insurance. I cannot imagine having to go back to work surrounded by new people every day because the lottery pool had the winning ticket and I wasn't in it. "What's that, Mr. Boss? Why am I not getting any work done? Maybe because all my energy is focused on trying not to kill myself."

Institutionalization

There are always the sad stories of those individuals that have become institutionalized. People that have been in prison most of their lives can become institutionalized. That is to say, they no longer know how to function in the outside world. Once released, they either find ways to get back into prison or commit suicide.

As we all know, jobs are a prison of sorts. The main difference is that you get raped metaphorically rather than physically. Sometimes, when a person has spent most of their life in this working prison, when they retire they don't know what the fuck to do with themselves. The drudgery that their lives had been is so ingrained into their very cores that the unfamiliar feeling of freedom from it is too much to adapt to. The most common result is that these people get another (gasp) job. Any retiree that ever admits to boredom should be forced to come back to their old job and let someone else retire. If you don't have any hobbies, your new hobby should be finding hobbies.

Exit Interviews

When leaving a job, you most likely want nothing more to do with the place. You don't want them wasting another precious minute of your time. Feeling this way, it may be the last thing on your mind to subject yourself to an exit interview. I say this is a golden opportunity to say all the things you were too afraid of to say while you still had a job. Now is your chance to give them a piece of your mind and tell them how you REALLY feel. Your boss was a wienie? The pay sucked? You and Bob liked to pee in the potted plants? Don't hold back, but if you still need to work make sure your next job is already lined up.

Sample Letter of Resignation

Dear Slave-Driving Shit-for-Brains,

I am writing to inform you of my departure. As this is a letter of resignation, I will tell you that I'm leaving because I've resigned myself to the fact that you and the rest of management are all ball-lickers, and this company sucks the aforementioned licked balls.

You have not received the standard two week notice because, quite frankly, you don't deserve it. As I was usually not informed of matters of importance until last minute and then forced to deal with it, I'm sure you'll have no problem doing the same.

I would like to express my sincere thanks for things like not being there when I needed help, keeping me overworked and underpaid, and for that crappy one-ply toilet paper. As a token of my gratitude, I stuck some of that one-ply to the top of your desk with my own feces.

There will be no need on your part to act as a reference. I

don't plan on getting another job, but if I did, I would have no need for my future employer to know I worked with such a group of hapless rejects. In fact, through drugs and therapy I plan on trying to forget it myself.

P.S. I nailed your wife.

10 Creative Ways to Get Fired

1. Show up, punch in, leave. Come back 8 hours later, punch out, leave. Repeat until fired.
2. Start a booger collection on top of your desk. If anyone tries to clean it off scream, "Don't touch my babies!"
3. Shave obscene words into your hair.
4. Keep offering to babysit your manager's teenage daughters while licking your lips and saying “Mmm, yes!” a lot.
5. Keep yelling "Are we there yet?" in a whiny voice.
6. Smash things you don't like with a baseball bat.
7. Pick a corner and designate it as your personal bathroom.
8. Wear shirts to work that say things like "fuck this place".
9. Speak only in belches.
10. Distribute copies of this book at work.

Conclusion - It Could Be Worse

"I think the person who takes a job in order to live - that is to say, for the money - has turned himself into a slave."
- Joseph Cambell
Is there another reason people take jobs?

Underdeveloped Suck

As crappy as your job may be, it could always be worse. Realizing that usually doesn't make me feel any better, but it's true nonetheless. It could be far worse. We've examined the suck of work from a relatively spoiled American perspective. The suck factor flies way off the meter in the less developed parts of the world. This chapter is dedicated to taking a glimpse into this uber-suckage. After reading this you'll probably still hate your job, but maybe once in a while you can remind yourself that at least you work near indoor plumbing and the beatings are minimal.

Getting a Job

In the 3rd world you don't find work, it finds you. There are no "careers" per se or even options. There's no circling want ads, no job sites to browse, or flyers to tear numbers from. There's just, "Hmm I wonder if I can do something for somebody to keep from dying" or my favorite, getting whacked in the back of the head and waking up at your new job.

There's no need for complicated applications or testing. Most of the workers are illiterate. As long as you look young and relatively healthy enough to withstand the torture, you qualify.

Interviews

If there actually were interviews, some of the questions might be as follows:

"How high is your pain tolerance?"

"Do you see yourself alive in 5 years?"

"If the worker next to you passes out from dehydration and exhaustion, would you notice or keep working?"

“Well let me ask you, how do you feel about oppressive heat and unbearable stench?”

“We’re looking for someone who will sacrifice their one and only life for pittance in return with no chance of improvement. My question, is that you?”

“Are you at least 6 years old?”

“Are you married to your fingers?, I mean, If you lost a few, would it be a major bummer?”

Starting Work

Getting to your job site initially might suck, but no worries after that because you probably get to live there. No morning commute, simply wake up on your wooden bunk in your smelly, crowded dorm, go eat your rice gruel and get to work!

Scheduling and Compensation

There's no complicated scheduling to worry about - you can expect to work EVERY day, ALL day. For your troubles, you will earn whatever the going rate of human exploitation is in your area. Forget about being able to afford to buy the stuff you're making for everyone else. And no overtime compensation, since no mater how long or hard you work it is never considered going above and beyond the normal requirements. The only beyond you can hope to achieve requires you to die to get there.

Superiors and the Rules

In this case, there may actually be people wielding machine guns. At the very least, people at the ready to beat you for looking up at your work station.

Rules are pretty straightforward - stop working for ANY

reason and get beaten, fired, raped, or shot.

Psychological Effects

They're bad enough that nets have been put up around buildings to prevent people from jumping. Perhaps it's corporate's way of saying, "Screw you, you're not dying until we say so. Now get off the roof and get back to work."

Since you don't make enough money to buy good meds or booze, taking the edge off I'm sure is a challenge. Perhaps since there are little or no safety regulations, you can unwittingly inhale enough toxic chemicals to catch a buzz. You also might get a high from the stimulants managers give you to keep working.

Amenities and Perks

- Break Room - room where they break your bones when you disobey orders
- Occasional food
- A beating to "perk" you up
- Restrooms - This becomes a problem of semantics because where you are forced to relieve yourself, if you are even permitted to do so, may not fit your definition of restroom. It may be a simple case of putting your excrement on or near the other piles lying around.

Small Talk and Cliches

There is no small talk because speaking to coworkers is strictly forbidden. But if they did spout platitudes, they might sound like these:

"Another day, another $1.25"

"Some monsoon we're having!"

"TGI...oh wait, nevermind. We work 7 days a week."

“There’s no I in team but one in WHIP!”

Customer Service

These poor people are usually serving us as customers which has to be the worst. You know how demanding people can be and they have to listen to it for 16 hours a day. You’re mad because you can’t figure out your new software and he is wondering if he can score some clean water.

Time Off or Leaving Altogether

Passing out, dying, or submitting to a beating are some of the ways to acquire time off. As far as leaving a job completely, it might be more accurate to call it "escaping." You just have to remember to zig zag to avoid the machine guns.

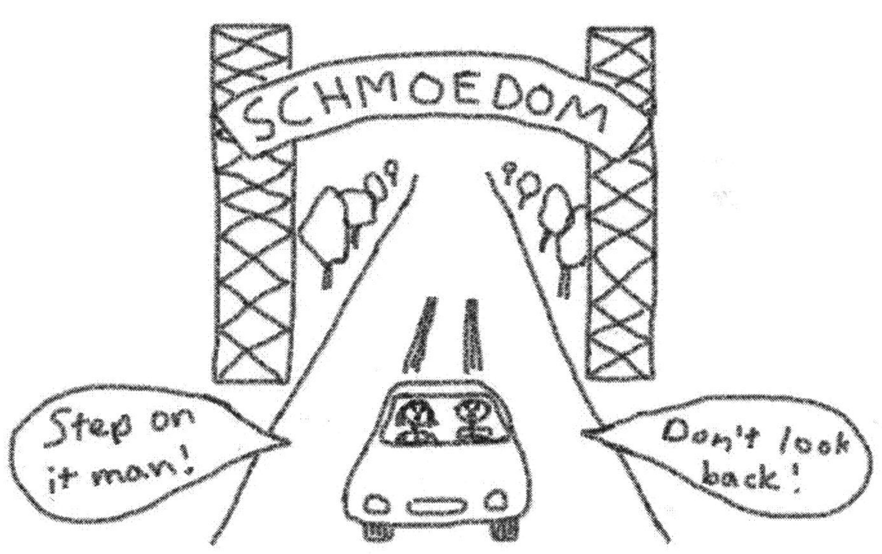
SCHMOEDOM
Step on it man!
Don't look back!

About the Authors

Summary

Kevin and Aaron are both experts in the field of mediocrity. Neither have ever fully committed to following their dreams or settling down into professional careers. Because of their fears, lack of motivation, genetics, the economy, and whatever else they can blame, their lives have been filled with schmoe jobs in one form or another.

Kevin Whelan

At fifteen, Kevin Whelan started his life in Schmoedom while working at a tire shop, stacking old cancer filled truck tires in the back of a trailer. After toiling in various roles as grocery store clerk, fast food worker, waiter, and dishwasher, Kevin went off to Marshall University in the fall of '95.

Five years later, Kevin had his education and was ready to hit the workforce with enthusiasm and false hope. Doing everything from substitute teaching to working on tugboats, Kevin plugged along from job to job going nowhere, where he remains today.

Kevin currently resides in Cleveland, Ohio with his wife and two sons. He is now working in human resources for a large company and writing as if his sanity depended on it.

Aaron Scardina

Aaron's official Schmoedom began early in life at the ripe age of ten. His foray into the working world started with the child labor scam known as a paper route. His three year tenure not surprisingly ended after the newspaper decided to have weekend deliveries in the morning.

Before jumping right into another job, Aaron became deeply focused on another endeavor, teenage girls. However, as one learns more about the female species, it becomes apparent that cash flow is necessary. Add a driver's license to the picture, and the occasional grass-mowing money was no longer cutting it, especially since he also started a grass-smoking habit. These factors combined with a nagging mother landed Aaron bussing tables at a Mexican restaurant. Now instead of inky hands he came home with "Mexi-hair". Throughout the rest of high school and during his collegiate debt-generating years, there was a smattering of random jobs ranging from washing dishes to wasting tax dollars for the U.S. Census Bureau. The highlight of these years was being fired from his job at the foreign language learning lab for reasons including, but not limited to giving orientations that sounded like a standup routine and suspicion of masturbation in the office. No comment on the authenticity of the latter charge.

After achieving a bachelor's degree that he had no intention of using to its full potential, Aaron has worked as a substitute teacher, adult toy party rep, bar back, weed whacker, painter, inventory counter, yoga instructor, standup comic, and delivery driver. He lives in Sharon, PA with his woman, just ten minutes from where he grew up. He's sitting there hoping people buy the shit out of this book so he never has to work again.

52619558R00131

Made in the USA
Columbia, SC
09 March 2019